Guthrie, Oklahoma:
Always a Railroad Town

Copyright © 2007
Joseph A. Cammalleri

Produced by:
Belknap Publishing & Design
P.O. Box 22387
Honolulu, HI 96823
belknappublishing@mac.com

All rights reserved. No part of this book may be reproduced or transmitted in any form or by any means, electronic, mechanical, photocopying, recording, or otherwise, without the prior written permission of the author.

LIBRARY OF CONGRESS
CATALOGING-IN-PUBLICATION DATA
has been applied for.

ISBN 978-0-9723420-6-3

For more information or to order additional copies of *Guthrie, Oklahoma: Always a Railroad Town*, contact:
J. Cammalleri
907 Koko Isle Circle
Honolulu, HI 96825
(808)-395-2212
e-mail: jcamma455@aol.com

Printed in China

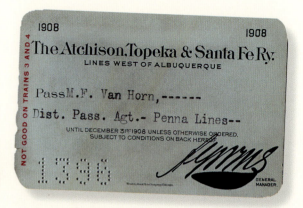

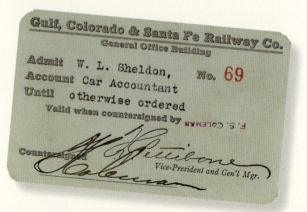

Vintage Railroad Passes from the author's collection.

Guthrie, Oklahoma: Always a Railroad Town

By Joseph A. Cammalleri

Belknap Publishing & Design
Honolulu, Hawaii

JOHN GILMOUR/GLEN MCINTYRE COLLECTION

Rock Island #741 at Kingfisher, Oklahoma, c.1906.

Contents

Dedication: Robert F. Read and Philip L. Moseley.. 6

Acknowledgements.. 9

Preface... 12

About the Author... 13

Chapter 1 – **Always on Track!**..15

Chapter 2 – **New Rails Roll into Guthrie: The Eastern Oklahoma Railway Company** 23

Chapter 3 – **Competition for the Santa Fe Railway; Choctaw, Oklahoma and Western;**

         The Rock Island and The Peavine..31

Chapter 4 – **More Competition for the Santa Fe Railway Company:** The Denver, Enid & Gulf Railroad.......43

Chapter 5 – **Tales from the Denver, Enid & Gulf (Enid District):** Personal experiences by Philip Moseley,

         Lester Terry, Keel Middleton and Phil Morrow..61

Chapter 6 – **More Steam Railroads come to Guthrie**: Choctaw, Oklahoma & Gulf; St. Louis & San Francisco;

         Fort Smith & Western; St. Louis, El Reno & Western; Missouri-Kansas-Texas.................71

Chapter 7 – **The Electric Lines of Guthrie:** Guthrie Railway; Oklahoma Railway Company................97

Chapter 8 – **Guthrie—Always on Amtrak?** The Heartland Flyer; DE&G Dinner Train....................103

Chapter 9 – **More Guthrie Stories:** Personal and Historical; Harvey House; Depot Restoration 109

References:..137

Index..139

Dedication

This book is dedicated to **ROBERT F. READ,** educator, historian, archivist and curator, owner of The Friday Store and Yale Depot Rail Museum in Cushing, Oklahoma, and **Philip L. Moseley**, retired railroader, writer, historian, and Guthrie resident.

Bob Read's father, Ezra Hart Read, served as station agent from 1933-1936 at the Santa Fe Railway depot in nearby Yale, Oklahoma, a station on the former Eastern Oklahoma Railway. Bob states that no one dared to call his father by his formal name, only as "E. H." This Oklahoma town was named as a tribute to the famous Yale Lock Company. Bob was born on July 22, 1920, in Cushing where he lived all his life except for three years service in the U.S. Army in Europe during World War II. After receiving his M.S. from Oklahoma State University, he became an educator and ultimately an assistant superintendent for the Cushing School District.

Bob bought the Yale depot after the station closed in 1969 and moved it to his residence in south Cushing. In 1981, he retired to devote full time to his Cushing antique shop and his Cimarron Valley Museum (the former Yale depot). Meanwhile, he collected numerous and incalculably valuable railroad artifacts, storing and displaying these in his museum. In addition, he purchased and displayed several railroad cars outside the museum, including a diesel switch engine, a rare box car, a 1917 oil tank car and a wooden Frisco caboose. Lanterns, railroad signs, caps, photos, timetables, rail cars, and other items were preserved inside the building. Bob participated in historic last runs and final train departures from Cushing, Kaw, Esau Junction, Skedee and other stations while leading the Cimarron Valley Historical Society as president for over 20 years.

Recently, Bob donated his irreplaceable rail memorabilia collection to the Oklahoma Historical Society for preservation and future display. In 2006, the Society honored him at a formal dinner while inducting him into the Oklahoma Historian Hall of Fame. In December, Bob served as a Grand Marshall for the annual Cushing Christmas parade.

As one of the most respected railroad historians in Oklahoma, Bob has provided significant data for both my current books. I was fortunate to first meet Bob in 1999 courtesy of Lawrence Gibbs and John Kirk, Jr. I have witnessed admiration and affection people feel for Bob especially at sessions of the annual Oklahoma City Train Show, held every first Saturday in December. During these events, an impressive number of attendees stop at Bob's display table to say "Howdy" and pay their respects.

Robert Read is an irreplaceable and important link to the rich railroad legacies of Oklahoma. Let us hope he continues to supply us with informative and heart-warming tales and data for many years.

Thank you for your devotion to rail history and your friendship.

COURTESY OF CIMARRON VALLEY PEOPLE, CUSHING, OKLAHOMA

Bob Read views Santa Fe Timetable while standing before his depot museum.

Philip L. Moseley was born in Douglas, Oklahoma, on November 5, 1946 one block from the former Denver, Enid & Gulf Railroad (DE&G) tracks. As an infant, he could hear the whistles of the passing Santa Fe Railway trains and would stand in his crib to peer at the action. He remembers the passing Doodlebugs (D'Bug) and steam engines with nostalgia. The northbound D'Bug drove through Douglas around 9:30 AM, while the southbound D'Bug rolled by at 3:30 PM. Occasionally, the Santa Fe would substitute a steam engine pulling one heavyweight Rail Post Office/baggage car (RPO) and a heavyweight passenger car for the D'Bug run. With sadness, Phil remembers his mother taking his older brother for a D'Bug ride to Enid just prior to the last run in 1951. He recalls that the D'Bugs and steam engines were gone in early 1952, replaced by blue and yellow Santa Fe diesel engines.

Thus, Philip became an ardent rail fan. In his youth, he "hung around" the Douglas depot helping the station agent by sweeping the platform and doing small chores. In return, he was trained in some of the basic operations of depot work. In the late 1950s he was befriended by **Vernon Yost** who worked as fireman and engineer on Numbers One and Two running in the Enid District. In his own words: "I was in hog heaven!" Phil and Vernon reunited in Guthrie to ride on the *Heartland Flyer* from Guthrie during the Amtrak trial run of 2006. Phil's family moved to Enid in 1952 when Douglas High School was closed. After graduation there, he signed on as agent operator with the Santa Fe and worked as a standby agent ("extra boards") at several depot agencies, such as Hillsdale, Oklahoma and Alden, Kansas. At the latter, he served as last agent on duty and helped close the agency.

Phil started his train service career with the Kansas City Southern Railway in 1971. His base was located in Shreveport, Louisiana. Unfortunately, he was forced to retire after suffering a disability in 1997 while serving as a train conductor. He moved to Guthrie, Oklahoma where he enjoys life as a legal researcher and railroad historian.

Via the Amtrak *Heartland Flyer*,
Philip Moseley, right, and Vernon Yost ride again!

With fondness, Philip recalls that his favorite operator job was working the swing job at Guthrie: *"I fell in love with Guthrie. As the first territorial capitol, it was rich in history, especially since it had been the largest railroad terminal in those days. Even in 1967 it was a busy place. Call sign GU saw many freights, a daily Texas Chief and a horde of grain trains in wheat rush days. I have felt blessed to experience the end of the age of passenger and mail trains. I regret having no experience with the steam engines, though. After retirement, I moved to Guthrie. These are the best years of my life and I am grateful for all this."*

Recently, Philip wrote several articles about his railroad experiences. These have been published in several rail related journals, including the "Wheat Rush" story quoted in this book in

EVAN STAIR PHOTO

a later chapter. Another article describing his last day at the Alden, Kansas depot agency is especially poignant. Philip had volunteered to become station agent at Alden, not knowing that the station was to be shut down in two weeks. On that fateful day, Phil was taken to lunch by the Santa Fe Railway official in charge. Since the local restaurant was closed, he treated Philip to a pre-wrapped bologna sandwich and a coke purchased at the Alden gas station/convenience store. Upon completion of this sumptuous feast, the "Brass Hat" generously informed Philip that he could take the rest of the day off! Philip accepted and used his employee pass to catch a ride to California in a Santa Fe passenger train.

Philip has been active in local groups advocating the expansion of *The Heartland Flyer* Amtrak train and resurrection of the old DE&G line. He has provided enormous encouragement and assistance for this work by gathering photos and data from historical societies and sending these to me. He has taken many photos of trains and historical places at my request. His friendship is most appreciated. May he see many trains serve Guthrie again!

EVAN STAIR PHOTO

All aboard! Amtrak's *Heartland Flyer.*

Acknowledgements

I am much obliged to the many fine people who aided and contributed to this work including:

Charles Albi, Gordon Basset, Art Bauman, Allen Clum, Russell Crump, Richard Dorman, Rick Duncan, Tom Elmore, Ron Estes, Ken Fitzgerald, Dick Fogarty, Gerald Forbes, Kenton Forrest, Preston George, Lawrence Gibbs, John Gilmour, James Levi Griswold, Greg Hall, Stan Hall, Robert Jensen, Marie Jones, George Janista, Tony Kassin, Jess Kelley, John Kirk, Jr., Tom Klinger, Terry La France, Glen McIntyre, Lloyd McGuire, Jr., Joe McMillan, John Mallory, Connie Menninger, Keel Middleton, John B. Moore, Jr., Phil Morrow, Bryan Moseley, Philip Moseley, Gordon Neff, Ron O'Dell, Christopher Palmieri, David Peters, Jerry Pitts, Robert Pounds, Bob Read, Maurice C. Rouse, David Sasser, John Signor, Richard Stephey, Evan Stair, Lester Terry, Norm Walters, George Watts, Evan Werkema, Sylvan R. Wood, and Matt Zebrowski.

Very special thanks to my wife, Rita Ariyoshi Cammalleri, for her encouragement, and professional advice and expertise in helping me finalize this work.

Thanks also to the following institutions for photos, data and advice:

Oklahoma State University Library
University of Oklahoma Library
Territorial Museum of Guthrie
DeGolyer Library, Southern Methodist University
Oklahoma Historical Society
Santa Fe Railway Historical and Modeling Society
California State Railway Museum
Colorado Railway Museum
Denver Public Library
Russell Crump's Santa Fe Archives
Microsoft Terraserver
United States Geological Survey
United State Department of Agriculture
Katy RR Historical Society
Frisco Railway Historical Society

GORDON NEFF COLLECTION

An air view of Guthrie, Oklahoma in 1970. Depot is in bottom left of photo.

Mock hanging at Guthrie, I.T. staged as a warning to claim jumpers.

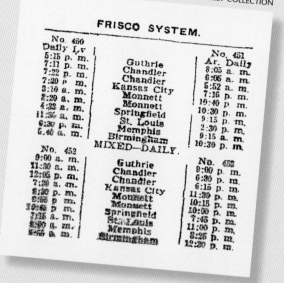

Eastern Oklahoma Railway construction train, c. 1900.

Eastern Oklahoma Railway grading crew. Local farmers were hired by contractors to grade the Eastern Oklahoma Railway. (See chapter 2 for more). 1899 photo from Santa Fe Railway archives.

Denver, Enid & Gulf Railroad boxcar 286, Guthrie, OK, c.1904. Note the truss rods between car wheels. These supported the car floor and kept the wooden body square.

Preface

Any railroad history of Guthrie, Oklahoma must mention the unique social, economic, political and financial forces that shaped Oklahoma Territory's settlement and growth to statehood. In the 1880s, only two major railroads, The Missouri-Kansas Texas (MKT or Katy), and The Atchison, Topeka & Santa Fe (Santa Fe) crossed from north to south through the Indian Lands-then called Indian Territory (I.T.), prior to the foundation of any major white settlements.

At the site of Guthrie, the Santa Fe constructed a wooden depot with the name "Deer Creek" on the west side of the main line track in 1887. This depot was located about 100 feet south of present day Oklahoma Avenue. The first water tank was located south of the depot with a water column added subsequent to construction of the brick depot. In those pre-Land Rush days, soldiers guarded the platforms when trains stopped at Guthrie. The military stood ready to arrest any unauthorized persons attempting to arrive in I.T. Passengers could board trains in Texas or Kansas to travel north or south through I.T., but were not allowed to leave the train anywhere in the Indian Lands without special passes. Of course, unscrupulous (or enterprising) individuals (who came to be known as Sooners,) ignored these edicts.

Two years after the Santa Fe Railway laid tracks, both Guthrie and Oklahoma City were settled officially on April 22, 1889, the first day of the famous 1889 Land Rush. Soon after, other railroads rushed in to provide freight and passenger service to both places. Most impressive for a small city, Guthrie was served by fourteen differently named railroads from 1889 until the movement (or kidnapping if you are a Guthrie citizen) of the state capitol to Oklahoma City in 1911. Gradually over time, the railroads left Guthrie. The St. Louis & San Francisco (Frisco) ceased rail service to Guthrie in 1905, turning it over to the Chicago, Rock Island & Pacific (Rock Island). The Missouri Kansas Texas (MKT or Katy) ceased service to Guthrie by 1924. The abandonment of the St. Louis, El Reno & Western by 1924 was more evidence of the severe decline of Guthrie's fortune. Over the years, excepting the Santa Fe and the interurban Oklahoma Railway, all other railroads terminated direct Guthrie train service. The interurban electric Oklahoma Railway terminated Guthrie to Oklahoma City runs in late 1946 leaving the original railroad, the Santa Fe, as the sole conveyor of rail traffic. Sic Transit Gloria!

In the 1990s, the Santa Fe merged operations with the Burlington Northern, forming the Burlington Northern Santa Fe, now called the BNSF Railroad. The irony emerges when one realizes that the Frisco, early arch-enemy of the Santa Fe, and one of the influential parties in achieving the movement of the state capitol to Oklahoma City, was merged into the Burlington Northern in the 1980s. Politics does make strange train fellows! Sick Transit, Gloria!

In alphabetical order, these are the various railroads that built and/or operated in Guthrie:

Amtrak
Atchison, Topeka & Santa Fe (Santa Fe)
BNSF
Burlington Northern Santa Fe
Chicago, Rock Island & Pacific (Rock Island/Peavine Railroad)
Choctaw, Oklahoma & Gulf
Choctaw, Oklahoma & Western
Denver, Enid & Gulf (DE&G)
Eastern Oklahoma Railway
Fort Smith & Western (aka Footsore & Weary)
Guthrie Railway
Guthrie & Western
Missouri-Kansas-Texas (MKT or Katy)
Oklahoma Railway
St. Louis, El Reno & Western
St. Louis & San Francisco (Frisco)

About the Author

Joseph A. Cammalleri was born and raised in the Bronx, New York City by loving parents and a great extended family. Despite growing up surrounded constantly by masses of noisy people and vehicles, he learned to appreciate solitude and peacefulness. He achieved these salutary states while serving two Air Force tours in Oklahoma, and even more so during two years of graduate study at Oklahoma State University (OSU) in Stillwater—by taking hikes across country.

To alleviate stress while studying for his M.S. degree at OSU, Joe hiked the thirty miles of the abandoned Eastern Oklahoma Railway grade, along the Cimarron River from Perkins to Guthrie. This experience in solitary splendor piqued his imagination and rekindled an interest in railroads he had acquired early in life. It was his good fortune to befriend several locals such as Maurice C. Rouse who provided him with historical data, photos and names of other people who could offer further assistance.

After graduation in May 1966, Joe served one and a half years at an Ohio Air Force Laboratory. The need for qualified combat air crews in the Vietnam War sent Joe to Tahkli Royal Thai Air Base in Thailand. His previous six-year tour of duty as a B-52 Electronic Warfare Officer served him well in performing duties while flying in EB-66 aircraft. He flew 100 combat missions jamming North Vietnamese ground radars in support of the F-105, F-4 and B-52 strike aircraft attacking targets in North Vietnam.

Joe completed his Air Force career after tours as an associate professor at the Air Force Academy and as crew stations supervisor for the B-1 Flight Test Team at Edwards AFB, California. During those tours, he published seven professional articles for scientific journals. Thereafter, he completed rewarding careers as a financial principal and academic dean and faculty for several California universities. During a lull in this period, Joe completed and published his first book: *Santa Fe's Eastern Oklahoma Railway Company—Book One: The Stillwater District*. The current endeavor is a predecessor for Book Two, a study of the remainder of the former Eastern Oklahoma Railway lines that ran between Pauls Valley, Oklahoma and Newkirk, Oklahoma.

The author has four grown sons, Anthony, Aaron, Thomas and Jeffery along with four grandchildren, Michael, John, Georgia and Isabel. He now enjoys life in Honolulu, Hawaii. His wife, an esteemed author, Rita O'Farrell Ariyoshi Cammalleri, her grown children, Daisy, Clare and David, their children John, Ashlyn, Shannon Bay and Ronan, along with boxer dog Cocoa provide loving companionship.

Joe Cammalleri, then and now!

Cottonwood Creek, 1889. Note the tent city and the folks rowing up the creek with a paddle.

One
Always On Track!

Boomer/Sooner! At first, July Jones was smug and pleased. After the train had stopped, he slid undetected off the supporting truss rods underneath the box car frame at a spot just north of the wooden Guthrie depot. Seconds later, the southbound steam powered **Atchison, Topeka & Santa Fe** freight whistled off, then clanked and chuffed on to Seward. Using the train noise and darkness for cover, he moved quickly toward some brush. At noon tomorrow, April 22, 1889, the Indian Territory would be opened legally for settlement by outsiders. July intended to stake out a choice lot close to the depot. In the gloom, he moved quietly through the grass. He found nearby Cottonwood Creek and selected a cozy hiding place along the east bank. Just as he was gloating with self-satisfaction, he heard rustling noises all around him. Damnation! Other *Sooners* were hiding alongside him! No matter, he could run faster than most and would beat all the others to that choice lot! When the bugles and gunshots sounded at noon, he would bolt from his hiding place, race across the tracks, pick up the lot stake, and make another mad dash to the Land Office to register his claim. Good luck and dream on, July! We will leave you to your *Sooner* fate.

AUTHOR COLLECTION FROM ROBERT CUNNINGHAM

Federal troops guard the trains at Guthrie, c. 1888.

Katy Railway Company common stock certificate.

Santa Fe Freight House and Crew, Guthrie, OK.

Sooners were the folks who slipped into Indian Territory prior to the historic opening of these lands to outsiders. Hundreds were caught and expelled, but many others successfully evaded the roving troops and staked personal claims. Still, thousands of law-abiding people lined up on the north and south boundaries of I.T. awaiting the signals to rush in and stake claims. Some Sooners died for their boldness. Quite a few sold their stakes for a quick profit. Others such as the Rouse family established permanent claims to establish farms in quarter sections in areas such as nearby Pleasant Valley in Cowboy Flat.

How and why had this historic land rush taken place? Much political and social agitation preceded this event. Two strong movements compelled settlement of I.T.: The American people pressuring the United States Congress, and the railroads' desire for expansion. The open land of Indian Territory was appraised as another opportunity for growth and profit. At first, Congress had forbidden the railroads to enter I.T. because it had been set aside as a sanctuary for the Native Americans (The Five Civilized Tribes) who settled there because they were forced to leave their original lands. Despite all the earlier broken promises and assurances, the U. S. government had declared Indian Territory to be sacrosanct. Surely the Paleface Chiefs in Washington would keep their word this time!

Denver, Enid & Gulf Railroad timetable, July 30, 1905. The line was first constructed from Guthrie to Enid. This sheet shows line laid to Coldwater, later named Hillsdale, and Nashville, name changed to Nash. This right of way was extended to Kiowa, Kansas, through Jet, Cherokee and Burlington. The Kansas City, Mexico & Orient road crossed paths at Cherokee with the DE&G. The Santa Fe acquired both lines, eventually. Note the name W. D. Blanton at bottom. He is mentioned by Preston George and Sylvan Wood in their epic work. Blanton Station, a junction where the DE&G and Frisco parted northwest of Enid, is named for him.

Conductors signal OK to leave.

OKLAHOMA HISTORICAL SOCIETY

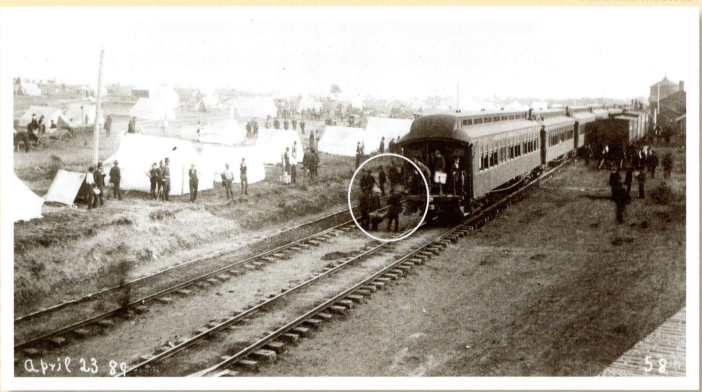

A southbound Santa Fe passenger train stops at Guthrie during the 1889 Land Rush. The original frame depot and water tank are on the west side of the tracks. The new Union Depot will be built across the tracks about where the five men can be seen (circled).

AUTHOR'S COLLECTION

Santa Fe Railway Company Gold Bond Coupon.

Nonetheless, on July 19, 1866, new treaties with the Five Civilized Tribes permitted one east-west railroad, the **Atlantic & Pacific R.R.** -later to be the **St. Louis & San Francisco [Frisco]** and one line going north-south, the **Missouri, Kansas & Texas** (Katy Railroad) to be laid across the Indian Lands. The Iron Horse's nose was in the Native Americans' tepee. In 1870, the Katy won the right to build a line through Indian Territory to the fabled Red River and Texas. The first Katy train reached Muskogee on December 21, 1872. In 1886-1887, federal edicts allowed the Santa Fe, using subsidiary **Gulf, Colorado & Santa Fe**, to build north from Gainesville, Texas, while subsidiary **Southern Kansas Railway** built south from Kansas. The rails were joined at Purcell, I.T., south of the future site of Oklahoma City.

GORDON NEFF COLLECTION

The Guthrie Santa Fe brick depot c. 1904. This structure became Union Station serving all the railroads operating into Guthrie. Note the many passenger baggage carts.

Santa Fe's Deer Creek frame depot and station quickly changed to "Guthrie" when the town site was named in honor of Judge John Guthrie, a Kansas jurist. The 1889 Land Rush made Guthrie an instant city and the Santa Fe depot became a key economic, social and political hub in Guthrie. In a short time span, forty passenger trains a day and numerous freight trains served Guthrie; probably totaling over a hundred movements daily, a noteworthy aggregate for a small, budding community.

In 1903, a new Santa Fe depot was constructed on the east side of the tracks. It was a formidable structure built with brick and other hard materials. (This magnificent building stands proudly today, thanks to the renewal efforts of owner Gordon Neff.) Soon, Guthrie depot became "Union Station" providing freight and passenger services for almost all the railroads serving Guthrie.

As the original line serving the Territorial capitol, the Atchison, Topeka and Santa Fe Railway quickly exploited every opportunity to expand services and profits. To encourage settlement, the Federal government had granted the railroad companies collateral land to establish stations and towns at certain intervals along the rights of way (ROW). After tracks were laid, the railroads sold the town plats to settlers. These cash infusions financed more railroad development. At the same time, adjacent towns were "encouraged" to donate land and cash to the railroads to help finance depot and station construction. Naturally, each railroad sought maximum control of the traffic generated from farms and businesses in the area.

Consequently, in 1899 the Santa Fe formed a subsidiary company to lay track from a new junction a few miles north of Guthrie eastward along the south bank of the Cimarron River. This corporation was established as **The Eastern Oklahoma Railway Company,** incorporated July 24, 1899 under the General Laws of the Territory of Oklahoma. According to *Railroads of Oklahoma*, the E. O. was the fourth railroad to incorporate in O.T., following the **Kansas, Oklahoma Central and Southwestern Railway** (1893), the **Gulf Railroad Company** (1896), and the **Blackwell & Southern Railway** (1899). In the next few years, other railroads constructed rights of way to serve the Territorial capital of Guthrie. Thus, the Eastern Oklahoma laid track at E.O. Junction, eastward toward Coyle and Perkins.

AUTHOR'S COLLECTION

Judge John Guthrie, Kansas Jurist.

Coyle Cotton Gin at Guthrie, Oklahoma.

Guss and Coyle's Eastern Oklahoma Railway Company land office in Guthrie. Campbell was renamed Pleasant Valley, Iowa City became Coyle and Iconium became a "Peavine Railroad" (Rock Island) station.

Two
New Rails Roll into Guthrie:
The Eastern Oklahoma Railway Company

Most probably, the Eastern Oklahoma was the last railroad constructed by the Santa Fe in Oklahoma by private contractors who hired local farmers using teams and workers to grade the right of way. The line ran from Eastern Oklahoma Junction to Ripley, with connections to Stillwater, Pawnee and Cushing. The first train ran to Perkins (Mile Post 30 on the first time cards) on January 1, 1900. The last regular freight train to Perkins and Stillwater ran in April, 1957. In May, 1957, a devastating storm system caused massive flooding of the Cimarron River. The bridge at Ripley and much track was washed out, causing the Santa Fe Railway to seek and obtain abandonment of the line from Guthrie through Perkins and Ripley to Stillwater. The Santa Fe continued operations from Stillwater to Pawnee until the 1990s. This line segment was then purchased by the State of Oklahoma and is currently operated by The **Stillwater Central Railroad**.

The Santa Fe used steam engines, gas-electric self-propelled cars and finally diesel locomotives to pull trains over this line. In the early days, Dr. Sylvan R. Wood rode along with train crews taking a plethora of photographs recording operations on the Eastern Oklahoma. His collection was purchased by Mr. Everett DeGolyer, prominent Dallas, Texas oilman who contributed it to the Southern Methodist University Library. The archivist there claims that the entire DeGolyer collection contains over 300,000 images.

Evan Stair photographed Stillwater Central engine 2186 at Stillwater prior to a freight run to Pawnee, c. 2003.

EVAN STAIR PHOTO

MAP BY MATT ZEBROWSKI

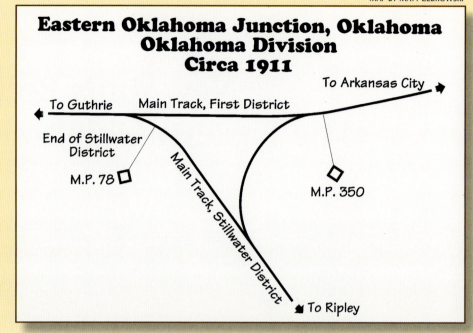

Eastern Oklahoma Junction was constructed in 1899 and dismantled c. 1970 by the Santa Fe Railway Company.

Two Santa Fe yellow-nose diesels await orders for a freight run to Pawnee from Stillwater, Oklahoma c. 1990.

Guthrie, Oklahoma, July 4, 2006: New meets the old. The red train parked on the siding awaits rehabilitation and a clear track to Enid (someday) to carry dinner riders. The BNSF train has a mixture of old Santa Fe and Burlington Northern painted engines.

Legendary conductor John Fogarty poses with the gang at Guthrie depot, c. 1910. Mr. Fogarty was one of the most revered public officials in Oklahoma.

Passenger and freight traffic increased steadily over the Stillwater District, peaking about 1924. Steady construction of highways and roads and growing use of trucks and autos cut into the passenger and freight business. By the 1950s the Santa Fe was actively seeking abandonment of this line. Permission was granted after the devastating 1957 Cimarron River flood. The tracks were removed from Stillwater south to Ripley, and west through, Cottingham, Perkins, Goodnight, Coyle, Pleasant Valley, and Russell. Only E.O. Junction and a couple of miles of track were kept in place to serve the Dolese Sand Company site on the Cimarron. Rouse told me that the Santa Fe set too high a rate for shipment and the Dolese Company business went to trucks. The orphaned wye, tracks and trestles were torn up about 1970. All that remains today are the hump of the south wye leg and a couple of trestle supports next to the section line road serving the sand extraction site. The ROW has been covered over by trees and brush.

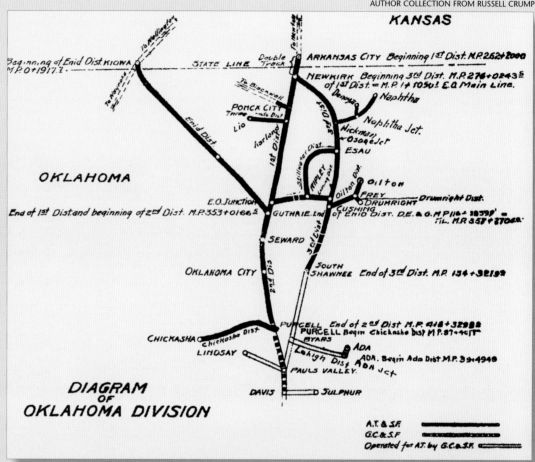

Chart displaying the Santa Fe lines to and from Guthrie, c. 1921.

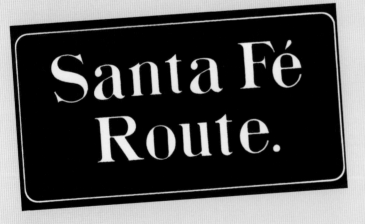

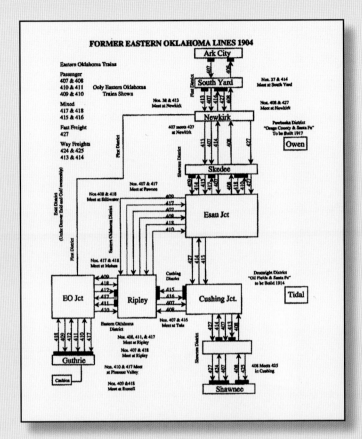

Traffic flow chart courtesy of Evan Stair.

Eastern Oklahoma Ry. Co.

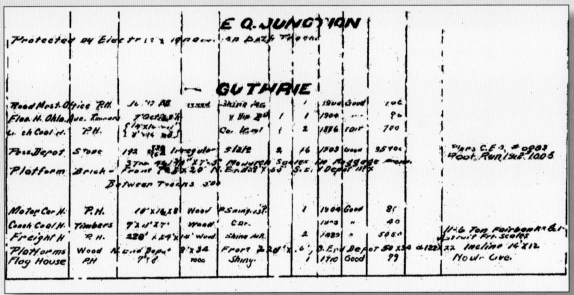

Structures record courtesy of Russell Crump.

TERRITORIAL MUSEUM

The first motel at Guthrie, I.T., April 1889. Note faithful old Towser!

COLORADO RR MUSEUM

Santa Fe stock car, Guthrie, OK, c. 1900. Note truss rods under car frame.

COURTESY OF GORDON NEFF AND PHIL MORROW

AUTHOR PHOTO

Football Special

to all five home games at Oklahoma University

Oct. 2nd — Navy
Oct. 16th — Kansas
Oct. 30th — Colorado
Nov. 6th — Iowa State
Dec. 4th — Oklahoma State

Football Special Schedule

Going		Returning*
8:00 a.m.	Lv. Arkansas City	Ar. 9:40 p.m.
8:20 a.m.	Lv. Newkirk	Ar. 9:00 p.m.
8:45 a.m.	Lv. Ponca City	Ar. 8:35 p.m.
9:30 a.m.	Lv. Perry	Ar. 7:50 p.m.
10:20 a.m.	Lv. Guthrie	Ar. 7:10 p.m.
10:45 a.m.	Lv. Edmond	Ar. 6:45 p.m.
11:45 a.m.	Lv. Oklahoma City (36th Street)	Ar. 5:45 p.m.
12:00 p.m.	Lv. Oklahoma City (Santa Fe Station)	Ar. 5:30 p.m.
12:30 p.m.	Ar. Norman (Brooks Street)	Lv. 5:00 p.m.

*Return schedule approximate. Train leaves 20 minutes after end of game.

$1.50*

Round trip chair car fare Oklahoma City—Norman

Other round trip fares:

Arkansas City $7.60
Newkirk 7.08*
Ponca City 6.37*
Perry 4.53*
Guthrie 2.80*
Edmond 1.83*

(*Includes Okla. sales tax)
Please note football ticket not included.

See your local Santa Fe agent or traffic representative for tickets and information.

Santa Fe

Riding the football special trains were social events in themselves.

Dick Fogarty at the John Fogarty residence, December 1967. Dick introduced me to Engineer James Levi Griswold.

1904 Eastern Oklahoma Railway timetable.

AUTHOR COLLECTION

COURTESY OF TERRITORIAL MUSEUM AND PHILIP MOSELEY

Logan County Map c. 1908

Three
Competition for the Santa Fe Railway; Choctaw, Oklahoma and Western; The Rock Island and The Peavine

Other railroads and business interests quickly recognized the importance of serving Guthrie, the first capital of Oklahoma. To avoid track duplication, directors of the **Chicago, Rock Island & Pacific** and the Santa Fe, made an agreement in 1899 to jointly build and operate a line from Kingfisher, Oklahoma to Seward, using the Santa Fe main line to reach Guthrie. That year, Santa Fe president Edward P. Ripley visited Guthrie to make a decision about building a new Union depot to handle the increasingly heavy rail traffic there. All problems resolved, the Rock Island constructed the line from Kingfisher to Cashion starting February 19, 1900. Cashion, named for Roy Cashion, the first Oklahoma soldier to die in the Spanish-American War, was opened for settlement on April 26, 1889.

Contractors Wogan and Calligan began grading with seventy-five teams of horses and a large work force. The Santa Fe, responsible for line construction westward from Seward to Cashion, incorporated the **Guthrie & Western Railway Company** on January 9, 1900 and commenced grading on March 1, 1900. The line was operated jointly by both roads over the years. The Rock Island extended service on this line, later dubbed **"The Peavine"** from Guthrie to Chandler, Oklahoma through Iconium, Dudley and Merrick.

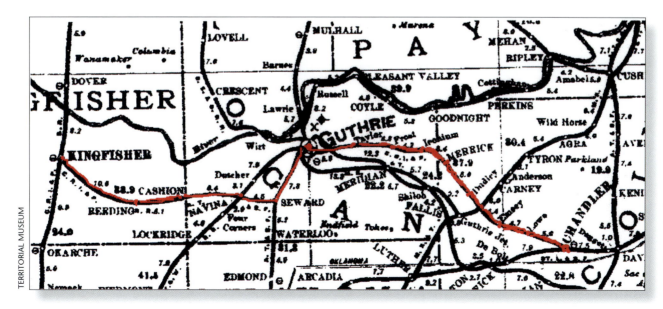

Guthrie area map showing the Peavine line running from Kingfisher to Chandler c.1912.

The first train chuffed over the line on May 29, 1900. The Rock Island ran an excursion train to Cashion on June 12 and the line was officially opened July 30, 1900. Joint operation of the Peavine commenced after January 1, 1901. The original schedule included three trains east and three west on weekdays, with two each on Sundays.

However, the Peavine was not complete. The Chandler citizens wanted their town connected to Guthrie and Kingfisher. The connecting tracks were laid by the **Choctaw, Oklahoma and Western.** By June 16, 1903, Iconium, fifteen miles east of Guthrie, was reached. The final spike was driven on August 28, 1903. A special train ran from Guthrie to Chandler that morning, except for the final 2500 feet of grade. The passengers were treated to the sight of a track-laying machine patented by J. H. Roberts, completing the job in two hours. The train arrived in Chandler around 4 P.M. The final spike was driven by Miss Amy Walsh of Guthrie. Though complete, the eastern half of the line still operated under the Choctaw, Oklahoma & Western, (soon changing its name to **Choctaw, Oklahoma & Gulf**). However, on March 24, 1904 that company was conveyed to the Rock Island for the sum of One Dollar!

Thereafter, the Rock Island operated the entire line as a single division. Unfortunately, the important goal of having tracks reach coal and oil fields in Eastern Oklahoma and on to Colorado and New Mexico was not achieved.

Track mileposts included Kingfisher to Reeding, 10.6 miles; to Cashion 5.1 miles; to Navina 6.4 miles; to Seward 4.5 miles; to Guthrie 7.3 miles; to Bestin (Taylor) 5.8 miles, to Frost 4.8 miles; to Iconium 4.2 miles; to Merrick 3.4 miles; to Dudley 5.0 miles; to Emsey 4.4 miles; to Loew 4.7 miles; and to Chandler 5.0 miles. Merrick was created in August, 1903 and named for Judge James A. Merrick, the town site owner. Merrick had a large station grounds along with a two story depot. A cotton gin was sited directly across the tracks.

Popular demand notwithstanding, insufficient traffic damaged the financial health of this line. Little else but cotton was available for shipment. For example, Iconium had a cotton gin, office, scales and a station in a derailed Pullman car, but served only as a flag stop. For passenger service, an early period Rock Island timetable might note that a train left Chandler at 8 A.M., stopped in Guthrie, and arrived in Kingfisher at 4 P.M. A departing train left Kingfisher at 11:30 A.M., arrived in Guthrie and terminated at Chandler at 5:15 P.M. As Glen McEntyre noted in his fine article, "The **Peavine Railroad**," published in *The Oklahoma Historical Society Chronicle*: "The pace was leisurely but it was apparently fairly dependable."

S.R. WOOD PHOTO, AUTHOR COLLECTION

The crew prepares the Cashion Local engine at Guthrie, OK, 1934. Neither the line nor the 4-6-0 engine would survive much longer.

Cashion, Oklahoma air view, 1995. USGS. Note RR grade at bottom edge of town (arrows).

PHILIP MOSELEY COLLECTION

GUTHRIE & WESTERN RAILWAY.					
No. 145	No. 143	Mls	STATIONS.	No. 144	No. 146
†8 10 A M	†2 30 P M	0	lve......**Guthrie**......arr.	1 15 P M	7 10 P M
8 40 "	2 50 "	7.3	" ....Seward....... "	12 54 Noon	6 44 "
8 57 "	3 03 "	11.5	" ....Navinia...... "	12 41 "	6 27 "
9 22 A M	3 22 P M	17.9	arr......**Cashion**.....lve.	†1222 Noon	†6 01 P M

An early Santa Fe timetable showing ATSF passenger operations on their portion of the Peavine Railroad.

OKLAHOMA DIVISION—Continued.

Dist. from Chicago, via St. Joseph.	Dist. from Kansas City.	Dist. from St. Joseph.	Station Numbers	STATION.	Telegraph Calls	AGENT.
894.9	377	398	S 227	Darlington ..Okla.	....	....
897.3	379	401	S 229	Rock Island Junct....	....	....
897.6	380	401		North Junct.	....	....
898.2	380	401	S 230	El Reno Yard	FT	....
899.5	382	403	S 232	*El Reno		‡R. E. Palmer
				" Ticket Ofs	RF	
				" Div. Supt. "	NO	
				" Disp. Ofs "	DE	
899.6	382	403		Belt Junct...	....	
900.3	382	403		Pacific Junct.	....	
904.8	397	408	S 237	Powers...	UN	C. A. Wallace
908.6	391	412	S 241	Union City .	CO	J. R. Trisler
914.4	397	418	S 246	*Minco		
919.0	402	423	S 251	Harold....		
922.3	404	426	S 254	Pocasset ..	CS	J. O. Richards
926.2	409	431	S 259	Martin...		
932.7	415	436	S 265	*Chickasha	CJ	‡Geo. Firmin
939.8	422	443	S 272	Ninnekah ..	N	E. L. Joyce
945.5	428	449	S 277	Agawam ..		
952.4	434	456	S 282	*Rush Springs	RS	E. S. Cummings
961.1	444	465	S 294	Marlow ..	MA	G. W. Siever
971.9	454	475	S 304	*Duncan ..	NA	C. C. Coleman
981.5	463	485	S 314	Comanche ..	OM	J. E. Light
990.1	472	494	S 322	Addington ..	A	H. N. Roberts
996.2	478	500	S 329	Waurika ...	KW	J. A. Bowman
997.5	479	501	S 330	Waurika Yard	WY	Conn. Sou. Div.
1002.5	484	506	S 335	+Sugden	NS	W. A. Hotman
1007.0	489	511	S 339	+Ryan	RN	C. C. Caldwell
1015.6	498	519	S 348	+*Terral	SF	J. B. McMahon
				K. Red Rd Rr. Bdge.		Conn. C.R.I.&G. Ry. Rr.

BILLINGS BRANCH.

Dist. from Chicago, via St. Joseph.	Dist. from Kansas City.	Dist. from St. Joseph.	Station Numbers	STATION	Telegraph Calls	AGENT.
835.1	317	339	S 167	North Enid Okla.	....	....
844.9	327	348	SA10	Cropper ...	....	....
851.0	333	355	SA15	Garber ...	GB	H. C. Wilson
862.3	344	365	SA26	Billings ...	BI	W.C.VanArsdale

Coupon stations, full faced type.   *Day and night telegraph stations.
†Ticket agent.   ¶Freight agent.
*Mail crane.   ‡Stock scales.
§City express office.   ‖No express office.
+ C. R. I. & P. stations operated by Southern Division, C. R. I. & G. Ry.

OKLAHOMA DIVISION—Continued.

CHANDLER BRANCH.

Dist. from Chicago, via St. Joseph.	Dist. from Kansas City.	Dist. from St. Joseph.	Station Numbers	STATION.	Telegraph Calls	AGENT.
875.0	357	379	S 207	*Kingfisher ..Okla.	KG	F. Pittman
886.1	368	390	SC 11	Reeding ... "		Mrs.T.E.Quigley
891.2	373	395	SC 16	Cashion ... "	CN	E. C.Shoemaker
910.0	393	414	SC 34	Guthrie... "	GU	D. A. Rainsburg
916.5	399	420	SC 40	Taylor ... "		
920.7	401	425	SC 45	Frost ... "		
925.4	408	429	SC 49	Iconium ... "		
928.8	411	432	SC 52	Merrick... "		E. G. Haver
933.8	416	437	SC 57	Dudley ... "		
938.0	418	442	SC 62	Emsey ... "		
943.0	425	446	SC 66	Lowe... "		
946.9	429	450	SC 71	North Yard. "		
947.9	430	451	SC 72	Chandler ... "	AN	A. J. Macomber

MANGUM BRANCH.

Dist. from Chicago, via St. Joseph.	Dist. from Kansas City.	Dist. from St. Joseph.	Station Numbers	STATION.	Telegraph Calls	AGENT.
932.7	415	436	S 265	*Chickasha .. Okla. ‡	CJ	‡Geo. Firmin
942.8	425	446	SD 10	Verden ... "	CK	T. B. Higgins
951.0	433	455	SB123	Anadarko ... "	DO	‡H. G. Harvey
965.0	447	468	SD 32	Fort Cobb ... "	FC	F. H. Rowe
975.6	458	479	SD 43	Carnegie ... "	CN	C. D. Steininger
983.7	466	487	SD 51	*Mount'n View " ‡	MO	F. W. Fanson
991.5	474	495	SD 59	Gotebo ... "	BO	B. R. Crouch
998.5	480	502	SD 66	Komalty ... "	KY	Wm. Taylor
1004.9	487	508	SD 72	Hobart ... "	KO	‡A. B. Harding
1008.6	491	512	SD 76	Cahill... "		
1013.8	496	517	SD 81	Lone Wolf ... "	FN	J. M. Howell
1021.5	503	525	SD 89	Granite ... "	GR	E.M.Thompson
1030.2	512	534	SD 98	Mangum ... " ‡	NG	‡E. M. Higgins

Coupon stations, full faced type.   *Day and night telegraph stations.
†Ticket agent.   ¶Freight agent.
*Mail crane.   ‡Stock scales.
§City express office.   ‖No express office.

Rock Island Branch Line timetable showing the Chandler Branch.

While the eastern half of the line struggled, the western half enjoyed better business. Cashion shipped many commodities and had stockyards for sheep and cattle. The depot agent there also served as telegraph agent. All mail departed and arrived by train. A large overhead water tank served the steam trains of the day. However, due to declining traffic and poor financial times, the eastern half of the Peavine was abandoned June 1, 1924. The Rock Island argued successfully that the parallel tracks of the **Fort Smith & Western** and the Eastern Oklahoma Railway could provide sufficient service for the area. Subsequent failure of the cotton crop sealed the fate of this half of the line. Today, one must search diligently for any signs of past railroad activity where this portion of the railroad was located. The eastern half abandonment doomed all the towns west of Chandler. Sadly, Merrick vanished altogether after World War Two.

Operations in the western half changed dramatically. Rock Island trains ran only from Kingfisher to Cashion with the Santa Fe operating from Guthrie to Cashion. With no place to turn, trains had to run backwards to return to Kingfisher and Guthrie, respectively. In 1933, both railroads petitioned to abandon the line. Deferred maintenance, the Great Depression and proliferating use of motor vehicles had doomed the Peavine. The Fort Smith & Western crossed the Peavine at the town of Navina during this period. When that line was abandoned in 1939, Navina slowly vanished. A present day visit to that site reveals little evidence of habitation The last train ran over the Peavine on March 31, 1937, carrying a load of wheat.

The Peavine Railroad was doomed to failure for similar reasons that caused so many other short lines and branches to fold: Lack of population, commerce, industry, and ultimately business. No private corporation can remain viable if earnings are constantly lower than expenses. However, present day Cashion is growing and prospering. The current residents should take pride in their old railroad that helped build early Oklahoma.

Above right: Cashion depot with ATSF freight car in right background. Below: The hard to find Peavine RR grade at Cashion, 1999.

Guthrie aerial photo 1937, USDA, author collection. Note the numerous RR grades. At extreme upper left: ATSF main line, DE&G branching to the left while St. LER&W curves off DE&G. FS&W grade is heavy line north of town, while curved grade below is CRI&P grade.

Located at Guthrie was an example of a steam engine coaling tower ordered by the Federal government after taking over U.S. railroads in World War One. Probably never used. Destruction date unknown. One such structure still stands in Cushing, Oklahoma. Since the Oklahoma Division steam engines had been converted to oil burners, the towers were to aid in reverting to coal burning if oil supplies were disrupted by World War One.

COURTESY OF PHILLIP MOSELEY AND STEVE WARNER, GUTHRIE, OK.

Santa Fe engines and crews at Guthrie Roundhouse in 1910.

COURTESY OF CASHION CITY HALL

AUTHOR COLLECTION

Choctaw, Oklahoma & Gulf certificate.

White Christmas at Cashion, OK.

The long-gone Navina depot in 1904.

Navina Railroading, Then and Now

An aerial photo of Navina, Oklahoma by the USGS in 1999. Note El Reno & Western and Peavine grades in upper third of picture.

I drove to the site of Navina station in 2003 for this shot of an empty field.

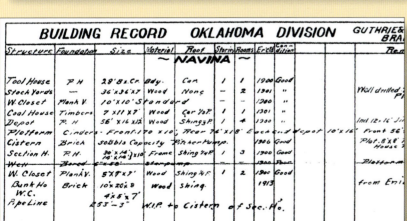

Navina structures record courtesy of Russell Crump.

Seward Railroading, Then and Now

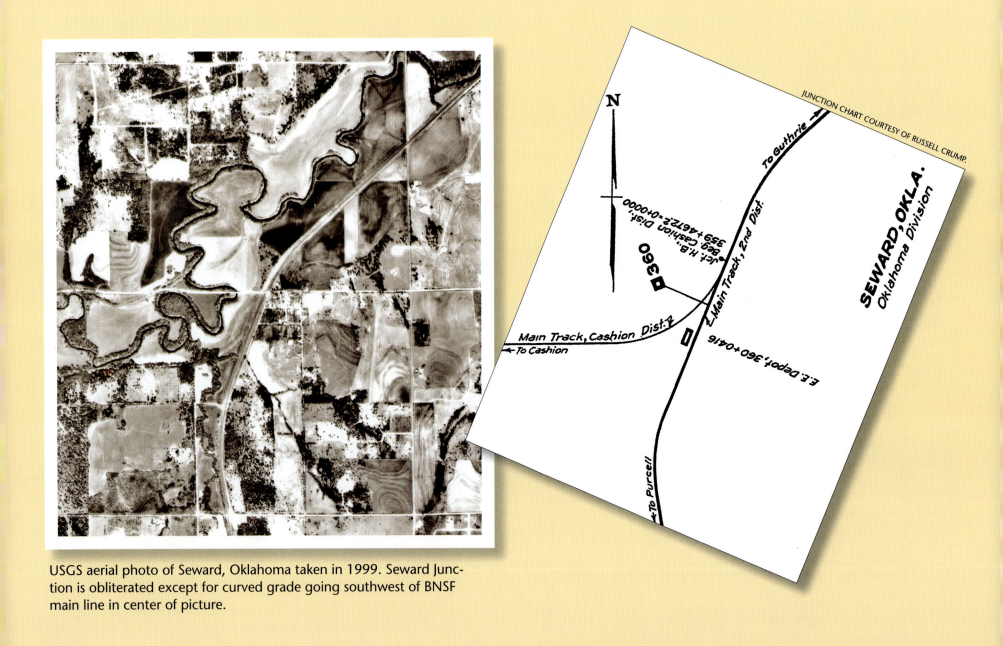

USGS aerial photo of Seward, Oklahoma taken in 1999. Seward Junction is obliterated except for curved grade going southwest of BNSF main line in center of picture.

The Seward depot stands in glory in 1931.

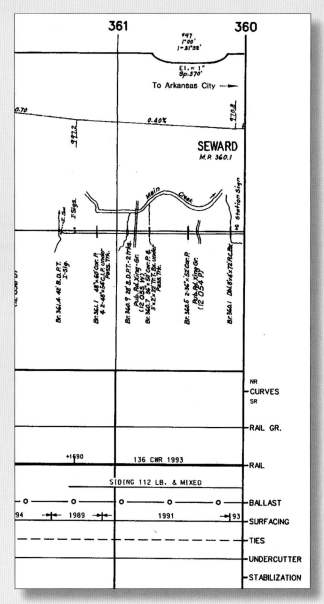

Seward Track Chart, courtesy of Russell Crump.

This is the site of the Seward Station in 2003.

AT&SF Ry. wood coal dock at Guthrie, OK, c. 1902.

Four
More Competition for the Santa Fe Railway Company

Competing area railroads cast envious eyes at potential business in the territorial capital when the Santa Fe and Rock Island started operations in Guthrie. In 1902, Mr. Ed L. Peckham, an Arkansas City, Kansas, attorney, started building a rail line from Enid, Oklahoma south to Guthrie. Two years later, he began extending the line northward to Kiowa, Kansas. This company was incorporated March 31, 1902 under an ambitious name: **The Denver, Enid & Gulf Railroad Company**. Such rhetorical chutzpah was affectionately preserved for years after the Santa Fe took over this line in 1907. Right into the 1990s AT&SF employees and Oklahoma old timers such as **Streeter B. Flynn, Jr.**, referred to the Guthrie-to-Kiowa line (Enid District) as "The **DE&G**."

The DE&G purchased only one new steam locomotive, engine No. 15, from the Baldwin Locomotive Works in December, 1905. Eight wheelers (4-4-0), ten wheelers 4-6-0) and moguls (2-6-0) spent time hauling freight and passengers on the line. Records show that Santa Fe motive power was supplied to the road as early as 1905. In 1907, the D.E. & G. was taken over by the Eastern Oklahoma Railway Company. A few months later, the parent AT&SF acquired all the assets of the Eastern Oklahoma line.

```
THE EASTERN OKLAHOMA RAILWAY, June 20, 1907:
   Newkirk, O. T., to Pauls Valley, I. T.                          183.57
   Esau Junction to Ripley, O. T.                                   40.24
   Guthrie Junction to Cushing, O. T.                               47.84
   Seward to Cashion, O. T. (The G. & W. Ry.),                      10.60
   Pauls Valley to Lindsay, I. T. (The K. C. & F. S. Ry.).          24.18
   Davis to Sulphur, I. T.                                           9.50
   Guthrie, O. T., to Belvidere, Kas.:
      Guthrie to Oklahoma-Kansas State line (The D. E.
         & G. R. R.),                                   113.01
      State line to Belvidere, Kas. (The D. K. & G. Ry.), 51.49    164.50   480.43
```

AUTHOR COLLECTION

Santa Fe Railway stock certificate.

Denver, Enid & Gulf Railroad Alfalfa Line logo, courtesy of Art Bauman and Philip Moseley.

GUTHRIE TERRITORIAL MUSEUM COLLECTION

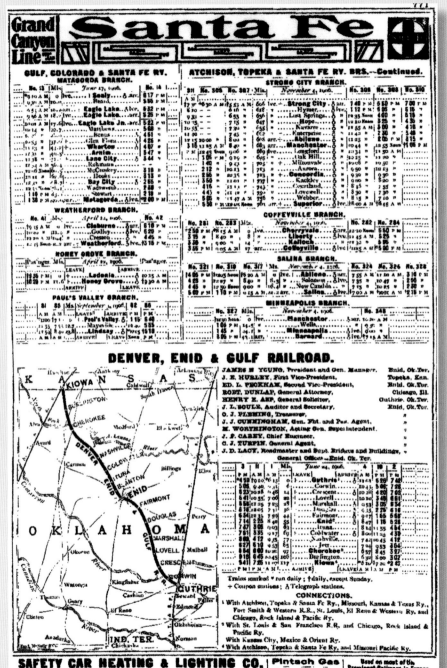

Denver, Enid & Gulf caboose.

DE&G timetable courtesy of Art Bauman. Coldwater and Nashville were soon renamed Hillsdale and Nash, respectively.

AUTHOR PHOTO

From Guthrie, running north to Enid and Kiowa, the DE&G trains passed Mudge station, ran over the Cimarron River bridge and reached Crescent, Oklahoma. Crescent depot stood proudly in 1966. It was torn down during the cost-cutting years of Santa Fe station agency closings. The first passenger train from Guthrie stopped here in 1902. The last passenger trains were Doodlebugs running in the early 1950s. I visited Crescent a number of times while gathering research for this book. It is a charming town hosting Kelly's Café located on Main Street across from the old depot site. We have a fond memory of Kelly's for its friendly atmosphere, good food and reasonable prices. When we mentioned the purpose of our trip through Crescent, the gracious owner gave us two souvenir cups at the end of our last luncheon there.

COURTESY OF JOHN B. KIRK, JR.

DE&G shops.

TERRITORIAL MUSEUM

The Santa Fe Station, the Gateway to Crescent, Oklahoma

While deficient in quality of reproduction, this copied newspaper photo of the first passenger train to Crescent is superb in historical content. This picture has been scanned three times, twice photo enhanced, enlarged and given loving care. We visited the Guthrie Territorial museum in 2003 and were fortunate to locate this photo in an old newspaper file.

Ken Fitzgerald shot this scene at Blanton Junction where the DE& G/Santa Fe left the Frisco Avard line west of Enid, in c.1972.

The Denver, Enid & Gulf R. R. Co.

USGS

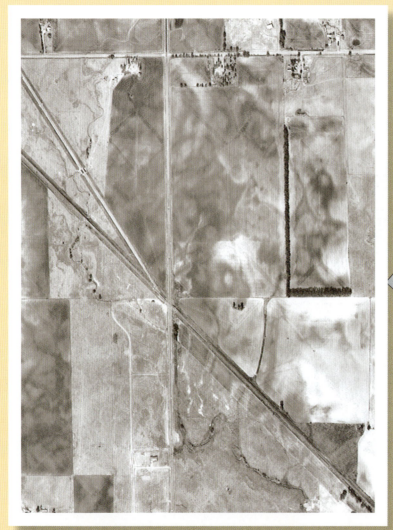
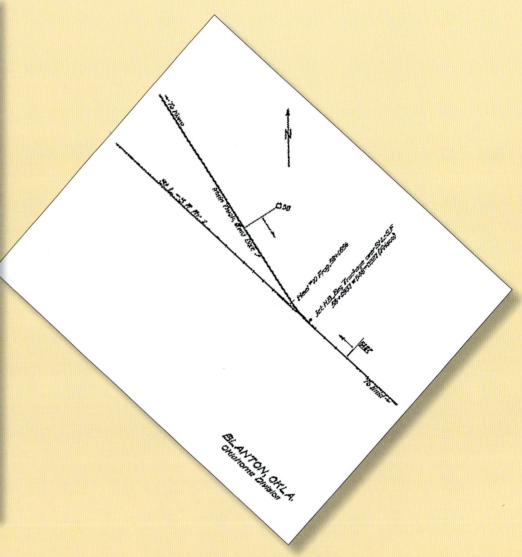

An aerial view of Blanton Jct. in 1992. Russell Crump provided the Blanton Junction chart at right.

Andrew Kirkpatrick / Guthrie News Leade

Burlington Northern Santa Fe employees remove a switch from the railroad tracks just north of Noble Ave. in Guthrie Tuesday afternoon. The switch once connected the main BNSF line to a line from Guthrie to Enid. The Guthrie Arts and Humanities Council has announced plans to use portions of that Guthrie-Enid line, which is currently owned by the state, for an excursion train.

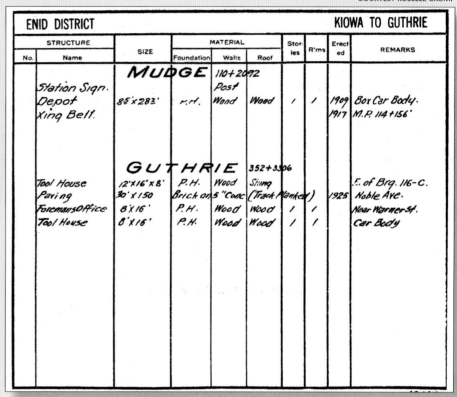

Gordon Neff and Phil Morrow supplied the news clipping at left in 2004.

Collection of John Kirk, Jr.

AT&SF No. 146 was DE&G No. 14.

JOHN B. MOORE, JR. COLLECTION

AT&SF (DE&G) depot is on the left, Frisco depot on the right, Enid, Oklahoma C.1922. R.B. Hughes evaluation photo.

JOHN B. MOORE JR. AND STAN HALL COLLECTIONS

The M-186 awaits orders at Guthrie prior to departure for Enid and Kiowa. John B. Fink photo.

AUTHOR PHOTO

JOHN B. MOORE, JR.

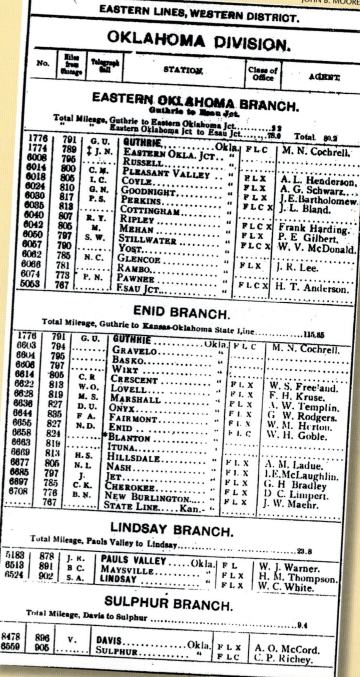

Mudge is the first station west of Guthrie on the DE&G. It was named for a Santa Fe official who worked in Topeka, Kansas. A couple of miles west the tracks cross the Cimarron River bridge to Crescent. Today, this station lies in a weedy overgrown area in desperate need of cleanup so it can accommodate the tourist dinner train being planned for the resurrected line! Just after I took this picture in April 1966, a track gang came by riding a speeder and a work car. I was asked to help replace a section of track just beyond. In return, the track foreman gave me a small sawed off section of rail to keep as a souvenir. I rode back to my car with the gang as a further reward. Only time I ever rode on Santa Fe rails!

KEEL MIDDLETON PHOTO

Santa Fe freight leaves Kiowa, Kansas for Enid and Guthrie, Oklahoma, c. 1990.

COURTESY PHILIP MOSELEY

Painting of Marshall depot on DE&G. Marshall was the hometown of Oklahoma historian Angie Debo.

WATER TANKS AND OUTLETS									
OKLAHOMA DIVISION									
LOCATION	SIZE	MATERIAL		CLASS OF TANK	ERECTED	REMARKS	KIND OF OUTLET	NO.	SIZE	ERECTED
		FOUNDATION	TANK						
		FIRST DIST.							
Arkansas City	24'6"x60'	cr. stone	steel	Treating	1909		Otto Crane	1	10"	1911
Arkansas City	24'6"x43'	cr. stone	steel		1900		Sheffield crane	1	10"	1896
Newkirk	24'6"x43'	cr. stone	steel	untreated storage	1904	Raised 4'3" in 1910	Otto crane / Otto crane	1/1	10"/10"	1906/1910
Ponca City	24'6"x36'	cr. stone	steel	untreated storage	1913		Otto Cranes	2	10"	1913
Perry	24'6"x45'	cr. stone	Steel	untreated storage	1906		Otto Cranes	2	10"	1906
Mulhall	24'6"x29'	cr. stone	steel	Treating storage	1899		Spout	1		
		SECOND		DIST.						
Guthrie	24'6"x45'	cr. stone	steel	untreated storage	1901		Otto cranes	4	10"	1919
Edmond	24'6"x29'	cr. stone	steel	Treating storage	1901		Spout			

OIL TANKS AND OUTLETS									
OKLAHOMA DIVISION									
LOCATION	SIZE	MATERIAL		CLASS OF TANK	ERECTED	REMARKS	KIND OF OUTLET	NO.	SIZE	ERECTED
		FOUNDATION	TANK						
		FIRST		DIST.						
Arkansas City	10'x38'	Frame Trestle on cr. stone	Steel	Delivery	1915	cap'y 465 Bbls.	unloading crane	2	4"	
Arkansas City	24'6"x43'4"	cr. rock	Steel	Storage	1915	cap'y 3490 Bbls.	unloading crane	1	6"	
Ponca City	24'6"x43'9"	cr. rock	steel	Storage	1915	cap'y 3501 Bbls.	unloading crane	1	6"	1915
		SECOND		DIST.						
Guthrie	10'x36'	Frame Trestle	Steel	Delivery	1915	cap'y 496 Bbls.				
Guthrie	24'6"x43'9"	cr. rock	steel	storage	1915	cap'y 3523 Bbls.				
Purcell	10'x35'	Frame Tres.	Steel	Delivery	1906	cap'y 465 Bbls.				
Purcell	24'6"x43'6"	cr. rock	steel	storage	1915	cap'y 3569 Bbls.	unloading crane	2	3"	1918
		THIRD		DIST.						
Maramec	10'x35'4"	Frame Trestle	steel	Delivery	1915	cap'y 465 Bbls				
Cushing	10'x35'4"	Frame Trestle	steel	Delivery	1915	cap'y 465 Bbls. Relocated 1916 from Tank Farm	Oil crane / Oil crane	2/3	6"/4"	

Both charts from John B. Moore, Jr. collection.

JOHN B. MOORE, JR. PHOTO

The Santa Fe turntable at Guthrie, Oklahoma, c. 1957.

AUTHOR PHOTO

The current terminus of the DE&G line near Fairmont, Oklahoma. The signals guard the tracks of the BNSF. The line was severed in late 1990s.

ART BAUMAN COLLECTION

The ATSF Kiowa, Kansas depot, terminus of the former DE&G.

KEEL MIDDLETON PHOTO

ATSF Kiowa, KS depot being destroyed on July 27, 2006. As seen from eastbound train H-BARKCK1-25 on engine BNSF 5243. Keel Middleton photo taken at MP 306.9 of the Panhandle Sub.

And on to Merrick, Oklahoma

GLEN MCINTYRE COLLECTION

The town plat of Merrick, Oklahoma. According to Glen McIntyre, nothing remains of the town that hosted a neat two-story railroad depot. Note the "C O &W" designation for the railroad right of way. Before I saw this map, sent courtesy of Glen, John Gilmour and Philip Moseley, we knew of another Oklahoma "COW" railroad, the Clinton, Oklahoma & Western. This "COW" evidently was the first to have a bovine descriptor. The track through Merrick was laid by the Choctaw, Oklahoma & Western from Chandler to Guthrie. Soon after, the railroad name was changed to Choctaw, Oklahoma & Gulf in 1902, shortly to be subsumed by the Rock Island Railroad. The Rock Island operated trains from Chandler through Guthrie west to Kingfisher on what was eventually nicknamed "The Peavine Railroad." Evidently, the Frisco had rights to run passenger trains from Chandler to Guthrie over this segment, also, turning over their traffic to the Rock Island in 1906.

Two views of Merrick depot c. 1907.

BOTH PHOTOS FROM GLEN MCINTYRE COLLECTION

Rock Island wreck on Peavine near Merrick, c. 1906.

Rock Island crane clearing wreck near Merrick c.1906.

The Rock Island Line

...was a mighty fine road to ride

Rock Island depot early 1900s.

The Kingfisher Rock Island depot c. 1950.

Stillwater District

Stillwater Central GP No. 2186 at Stillwater, OK, c. 2000.

C. 1990. Time grows short for passage of Santa Fe trains running in the Stillwater District. As Russell Crump stated so well, the Santa Fe was already "playing footsie" with the Burlington Northern by securing running rights over the Avard branch. Very soon, the Santa Fe will sell the Stillwater to the Pawnee remnant of the former Eastern Oklahoma Railway Company to the State of Oklahoma, and the Stillwater Central will take over train operations.

Five
Tales from the Denver, Enid & Gulf (Enid District)

Several people have furnished some enjoyable stories: two retired railroaders, Lester Terry; Philip Moseley, a still active BNSF engineer; Keel Middleton; and one dedicated rail fan, Phil Morrow. Lester, Philip and Phil currently reside in Guthrie, Oklahoma, while Keel lives in Wellington, Kansas.

Lester reminisced about a late-night freight run from Guthrie to Enid in the late 1980s. It seems that there was a dark stretch of line between Fairmont and Enid where a section line road ran close to the tracks. Sometimes this road served as a lovers' lane and the train crew would take delight in using a portable spotlight to illuminate the auto interiors and scenes of clumsy passion. One particular night, Lester, while standing on the walkway of the moving engine, aimed his light at a darkened parked car. The male occupant whirled round from his amorous actions, grabbed a handgun and commenced firing at the Santa Fe engine. Several shots ricocheted off the engine as Lester and the other crewmen ducked. Fortunately, no one was hit. The crew recognized the shooter as a cook and his paramour waitress who worked in one of the Enid beaneries frequented by Santa Fe crews. Only Lester knows the aftermath of this incident. But, talk about a Red Ball Express!

Philip Moseley served the Santa Fe agencies at Alden, Kansas and Hillsdale, Oklahoma before moving on to the Kansas City Southern Railway. He published an article in a 2005 edition of The Santa Fe Railway Historical & Modeling Society publication, *The Warbonnet*. It describes the frantic rail activity dealing with the harvest of wheat in the spring.

Wheat Rush Story
by Philip Moseley

The "Wheat Rushes" in Oklahoma in the past years were events that boggled the minds of farmers, elevator managers, and railroads. These annual events were unmatched in magnitude, unraveled nerves among railroaders and shippers and created for a few short weeks, a monumental traffic jam on the railroads. It was an event well worth experiencing. This story describes my experiences with "The Great Wheat Rush" that I hope you will find to be nostalgic and interesting from the railroad and grain business perspectives.

In 1966, I went to work for the Santa Fe Railway at agencies in Kansas and Oklahoma. Having grown up in Douglas, (formerly Onyx) Oklahoma, on the western Oklahoma prairies, I was well acquainted with the Oklahoma wheat harvest and the major event it turned into. The harvest period of two to three weeks in the wheat country of Oklahoma and the Texas Panhandle was a hectic time. Farmers would plant their wheat crop in August. The wheat would grow and even remain dormant at times, until spring arrived and the fun began with the start of the harvest. Long ago in Douglas, Oklahoma, I saw farmers cut wheat all night long and the grain elevators stay open all night long also. The elevator managers placed a red light on top of their silos. This light was not an aircraft warning light, but that the elevator was open and accepting wheat. If the light was out, this meant the

PHILIP MOSELEY COLLECTION

Hillsdale Santa Fe depot, c. 1907.

elevator was filled, a warning signal to let the farmers know the elevator was closed.

I served on the Extra Board in 1967 and 1968, and managed to bid on a few agencies on the Santa Fe. I was on the extra board working the AG tower and "Brownie Trap" (Demarits) on the main line of the Santa Fe between Emporia and Wellington on the Belen cutoff line where they were running trains like streetcars. I was working second trick at "AG" and already had my rear chewed in high form for delaying some "HOT SHOT" Santa Fe freights to allow a Frisco local to cross the interlocker. I would have bid for the third trick in Hell to get out of there. Just then, along came a bulletin for a "Grain Agency" at Hillsdsale, Oklahoma, not far from my home in Douglas. I jumped on it and made a bid.

Now at that time, the Santa Fe had quite a number of what was called "Grain Agencies" in wheat country. These were small agencies that were closed for the winter and opened only for the three or four weeks of harvest every May and June.

Hillsdale is a small town on the former Enid District of the Santa Fe Railway, originally part of the old Denver, Enid & Gulf Railroad that the Santa Fe took over in 1907. Two local freights ran through Hillsdale, Numbers 181 and 182. During the winter, if they had 35 or 40 cars, they were big trains.

Enid, Oklahoma was always the center of the Wheat Rush. Enid was nicknamed the "Wheat Capital of the World" because it had the greatest wheat storage in the number and capacity of elevators there. Hutchinson, Kansas had the world's largest grain elevator, but Enid topped it with greater total wheat storage. These were owned and operated by the likes of Union Equity, Pillsbury, Johnson Mills, Enid Terminal Elevator, General Mills and a few others.

At that time, Enid was served by three railroads, the Santa Fe, Rock Island and the Frisco. These railroads made an agreement to share the switching of the various elevators. One year the Santa Fe would switch, the next year, the Frisco would switch, then the Rock Island the year after and so on.

Branch and main line business for the railroads would explode when harvest began. The main lines of all three railroads in Kansas, Texas and Oklahoma were busy because local freight traffic increased from winter locals running every other day, to two or more locals running daily each way with as many cars as they could haul-100 to 125 cars or more! Cars would be in short supply and covered hoppers were just starting to be used. Many elevators still used old box cars that they coopered by nailing wooden and paper doors in order to hold the wheat. Many times, the elevator managers would order say six empty covered hoppers for wheat loading and due to the car shortage, might get three cars. Even the grain box cars were in short supply.

All three railroad yards at Enid plus the elevator yards stayed plugged for extended periods. Due to the amount of business, the railroads could not return the empties fast enough to get back in line. This made the elevator managers antsy. If they could not get enough freight cars to carry out the wheat, the elevators would be filled. The overflow wheat would have to be piled on the ground. This was costly to everyone, because if it rained, the wet grain tended to spoil and be ruined. Grain dryers would be used to save this wheat, an extra cost.

While I worked Hillsdale, Local No.'s 181 and 182 would haul empty grain hoppers north, working the various elevators to gather as many cars as they could handle. They would set out a bunch of empty cars at Cherokee to be sent down the old Santa Fe Orient District through western Oklahoma and Texas over Arthur Stilwell's old Kansas City, Mexico & Orient Railroad. The remaining cars would be taken to Kiowa, Kansas for distribution. No. 181 South would pick up grain at Kiowa, then from Cherokee from the Orient District and more wheat from Hillsdale and other stations. If possible these trains were loaded to full tonnage and would highball through the stations making nervous antsy elevator operators demanding to know why they were bypassed. Second sets of trains would be run to ease the loading problems.

Adding to the madness, trains would leave Enid with as many cars as they could handle, mostly empty hoppers and grain boxes, arrive at Cherokee and have to set out most of them for Orient line shipment. The remaining cars would be taken to Kiowa to be lined up. There, train would pick up loaded wheat hoppers and boxes, so many that by the time the trains reached Hillsdale, many could not stop to pick up any more cars because they were loaded to full tonnage. At Hillsdale, I watched trains pulled by seven or eight "F" units pulling over 100 loaded cars, sanders on the engines wide open, throttles in Number Eight position (maximum) doing all of ten miles per hour, pulling to the limit. Now multiply all of this by the number of branch lines in Oklahoma, Kansas and parts of Texas, and you can really see what a grand event the "Wheat Rush" was: Three late spring weeks that boggled the mind and wore nerves thin on the railroads.

I worked the Hillsdsale agency for a total of three weeks.

RAIL IMAGES/RON ESTES

Santa Fe F "Covered Wagon" 1706 at Cherokee on Orient District with Texas Chief, c.1972.

I was glad to be part of the wheat rush and experience the MADHOUSE on the railroads. It was quite interesting, to say the least. Currently, the wheat rushes in Oklahoma and Kansas are different and do not create the rail traffic jams of the past. There are excess numbers of hoppers available, although the grain boxes are gone. Most of the wheat is now trucked from towns like Hillsdale, Douglas and Lovell to Enid. After purchase there, the wheat is loaded into 100 covered hopper unit grain trains and shipped to Galveston, Texas for export. Hutchison, Wichita and Kansas City export wheat traffic is handled the same way.

The old Enid District (DE&G RR) is now all but abandoned. The line from Blanton Junction to Cherokee and Kiowa was taken up. The wye remains at Kiowa along with about a mile of track for car storage. The Orient line was taken up north of Thomas, Oklahoma and Cherokee now has no railroads. All Enid grain is now shipped over the old Frisco line to Perry, Oklahoma and then down to the Gulf via the BNSF (old Santa fe) from there. The line from Guthrie to Enid is in place, but needs rehabilitation if it is reopened. All the small depots along the line are now gone, and like the steam engine, passenger trains and telegraph, the "Wheat Rushes" are now just a part of history.

PHILIP MOSELEY PHOTO

The depot at Douglas, Oklahoma.

Enid District Memories
by Keel Middleton

The trains that I worked were the 476 and 674. They were put on the schedule in late 1990 to move the UPS to and from Oklahoma City to the west, while finished autos also went west with a few empty racks going east. This train ran over the Waynoka Sub between Avard and Waynoka, giving us mileage equalization twice a year while the job lasted. The Arkansas City crews had seniority for this job. It lasted about two years if my memory serves me right. I ran there for a week in February 1991. As far as jobs go, it was a good one, but since our home terminal is Wellington, Kansas, it was too far away as Wellington lies 140 miles from Oklahoma City. I stayed in Oklahoma City for the week I worked the job and went rail fanning when I had the chance.

The job began at 10 A.M. at the General Motors yard, four miles from the main line. We picked up our power and ran over to Flynn Yard to pick up our train. This was done because Flynn Yard lacks a good diesel facility. Not really a good arrangement. We usually didn't depart until Noon for Guthrie to pick up cars from Ark City or Tulsa off the Burlington Northern (BN) connection at Perry.

We normally left Guthrie about 1:30 P.M., stopping at Crescent about 2 P.M. We would stop there and head to the Convenience Store just north of the tracks for a snack. We would buy broasted chicken and sandwiches that were micro-waved and have a picnic on the way to Enid. The train normally had about 40 cars out of Guthrie. We did no work between Guthrie and Enid. At Enid, we made a set out and pick up, then headed to Avard over the BN, again doing no work. At Waynoka, we separated the TOFC traffic for a westbound pick up, usually the 188 train that arrived Waynoka at 8 P.M. If the traffic was just right, sometimes the 698 train would follow us across the BN and would make the pick up at Waynoka.

The 647 went back on duty at Waynoka after all the eastbounds had set out and we had gotten our rest, usually around 2 A.M. We then built our own train and headed east with an Enid set out and the Oklahoma City UPS traffic. The Enid set out headed east was usually greater than the one going west. We usually got a big fill at Enid, also. This train was blocked the Oklahoma TOFC cars on the rear, so as the train pulled into Flynn yard, a switch engine grabbed the cars and spotted them on the TOFC ramp. The cars were unloaded before we reurned the power back to the GM yard. With the right timing, we could reach Crescent for breakfast. That store opened at 6:30 A.M. so we usually waited for a few minutes to get chow such as doughnuts and micro-waved breakfast sandwiches that were always good. Then, off to Guthrie where we usually had no work going to Oklahoma City. Again, there was no other work on the Enid sub.

It was not long after I left that line that a fatal crash took place at Fairmont. Due to fog, the ATSF crew became disoriented and did not see the approach signal for the BN crossing. Sure glad I wasn't there when that happened around April, 1991 to my best recollection.

District track speed was timetable posted at 49 MPH in 1991, but we had a slow order restricting us to 40 MPH, and to 25 MPH through Marshall and Douglas. The track wasn't that bad. The grade just needed some ballast and tamping to get it back in shape.

That job basically spelled the end of the line for the Enid to Kiowa part of the Enid sub. Traffic moved to Waynoka where it was easier to pick up cars than at Kiowa. Only a few harvest jobs and extras worked between Kiowa and Enid after the 476/674 trains were stopped. Of course, the 1993 flood took out the Enid District, so the ATSF obtained trackage rights from the BN between Enid and Perry, spelling the end for the Enid District line.

If you are wondering about the power used for the 476/674 trains, it was anything we could get. We put a GP-7 in the middle for tow trips and No. 9500, an SF30C on one end with a GP-35 on the other end. On one trip, we used a GP-40X in the consist. Another time we used a GP-20 for a westbound trip. On one of the trips, it rained almost the entire run, so I did not get out and shoot much from the engine. We took the siding at McWillie west of Enid on another trip to wait for the 856 train to pass us. Trains running between Enid and Guthrie tended to use bigger power if we could get it. In the late '80s, trains between Kiowa and Enid usually rated four axle power, usually GP-38, GP-39-2, and B-23-7. In the late 1970s, the Enid to Kiowa local rated GP-7 and CF-7 on a regular basis.

I remember my first trip to Clinton, driving there from Blackwell with the other brakemen. We drove through Jet where we saw the Enid local using four GP-7s and two F-7Bs for power. I was a new guy and hesitated to ask if we could stop so I could take a photo. Always wished I had done that. The train was headed for Kiowa with a long string of cars. Some of these cars were bound for Cherokee for us to pick up later on our trip from Clinton to Altus.

I also remember the Burlington siding being full with auto racks for the GM plant. This was about 1979. The Enid crew told me that they had racks stored all over the Enid District that year. Passing through Cherokee, we saw the south pass (southeast of the depot) full of racks, also.

PRESTON GEORGE PHOTO

Rock Island 3031 at Enid, Oklahoma, date unknown.

Phil Morrow has collected all sorts of Santa Fe memorabilia relating to the Guthrie operations. He loaned me some forms salvaged from the closing of that agency. Some are desultory, others are humorous and a few are quite serious. In one instance, a child was traveling alone on the *Texas Chief*. The little girl missed her stop causing all sorts of anxious activity and concern. In another instance, a crew man was needed for an Enid District run. Frantic searches of local hotels, bars and eating houses ensued. At the last minute, someone discovered the hunted man asleep in his pickup truck parked next to the depot. We are missing all these interesting activities in our modern quest for speed.

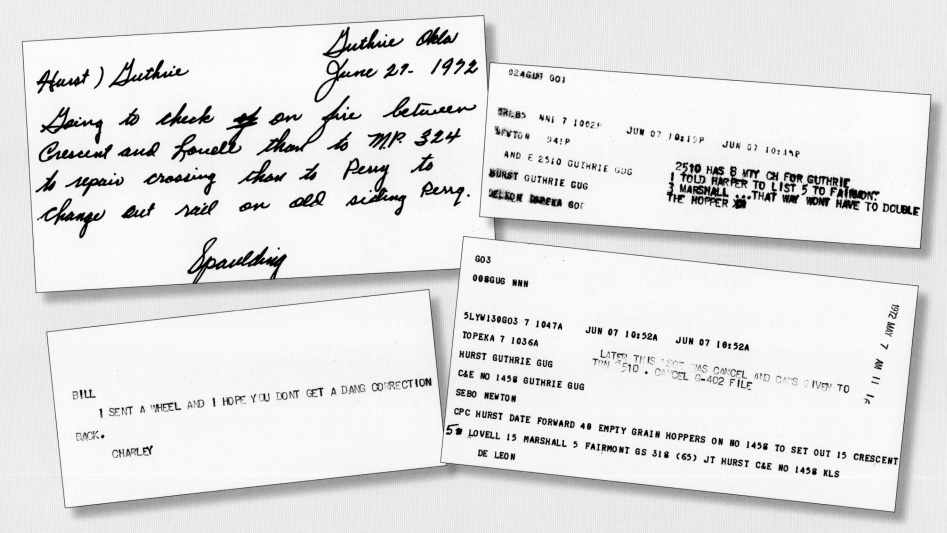

```
YJ1       WHL NNN 010 001 GUG

(5JEP900 09 315A    JUN 09 03:16A    JUN 09 03:38A

);1475H1       247LW1060822359WN 1687Y420

001ATSF999341WCE         1808      30         - 1687 1808INSERVICE
002UTLX 88175  TE        5081      30         - 1687 1808CUSHINGTANKCAR
003UTLX 38739  TE        5081      30         - 1687 1808CUSHINGTANKCAR
004UTLX 38497  TE        5081      30         - 1687 1808CUSHING TANK CA CO
005UTLX 89322  TE        5081      30         - 1687 1808CUSHINGTANKCAR
006UTLX 10344  TE        5081      30         - 1687 1808CUSHINGTANKCAR
007UP    13112CHLSASH    5485      130100     - 1687 1808BROCKWAYGLASS
008NATX 34898  TE        5081      45         - 1687 1808CUSHINGTANKVAR
009UTLX 37888  TE        5081      45         - 1687 1808CUSHINGTANKCAR
010GATX 91886  TE        5081      30         - 1687 1808CUSHINGTANKCAR
011UTLX 99010  TE        5081      30         - 1687 1808CUSHINGTANKCAR
012UTLX 89287  TE        5081      30         - 1687 1808CUSHINGTANKCAR
013GATX 91864  TE        5081      30         - 1687 1808CUSHINGTANKCAR
014SLSF333035M4LBUTTER   5437      90 50      - 1687 1808HARPS FARMS    MR
015ATSF 734046ME32       5081      30         - 1687 1808DELONSG294
016ATSF 735866ME32       5437      30         - 1687 1808AGENT
017ATSF 732336ME42       5437      30         - 1687 1808AGENT
018ATSF 11098A5LRAPER    5437      48 18      - 1687 1808CHWNLSECO
019SP    692661 RLBEER   6050      110 58     - 1687 1808J K BOERSMA
020CBQ   93027F5LLUMBER  5437      80 50      - 1687 1808BISONLUMBER
021ATSF301514CHLWHT      5437      132100     - 1687 1808SHAWNEEMLGCO
022ATSF305541CHLWHT      5437      131100     - 1687 1808SHAWNEEMLGCO
023ATSF307529CHLWHT      5437      132100     - 1687 1808SHAWNEEMLGCO
```

ATSF Guthrie Car Loading Sheet

Santa Fe local near Yost, Oklahoma, c. 1992

PHIL MORROW COLLECTION

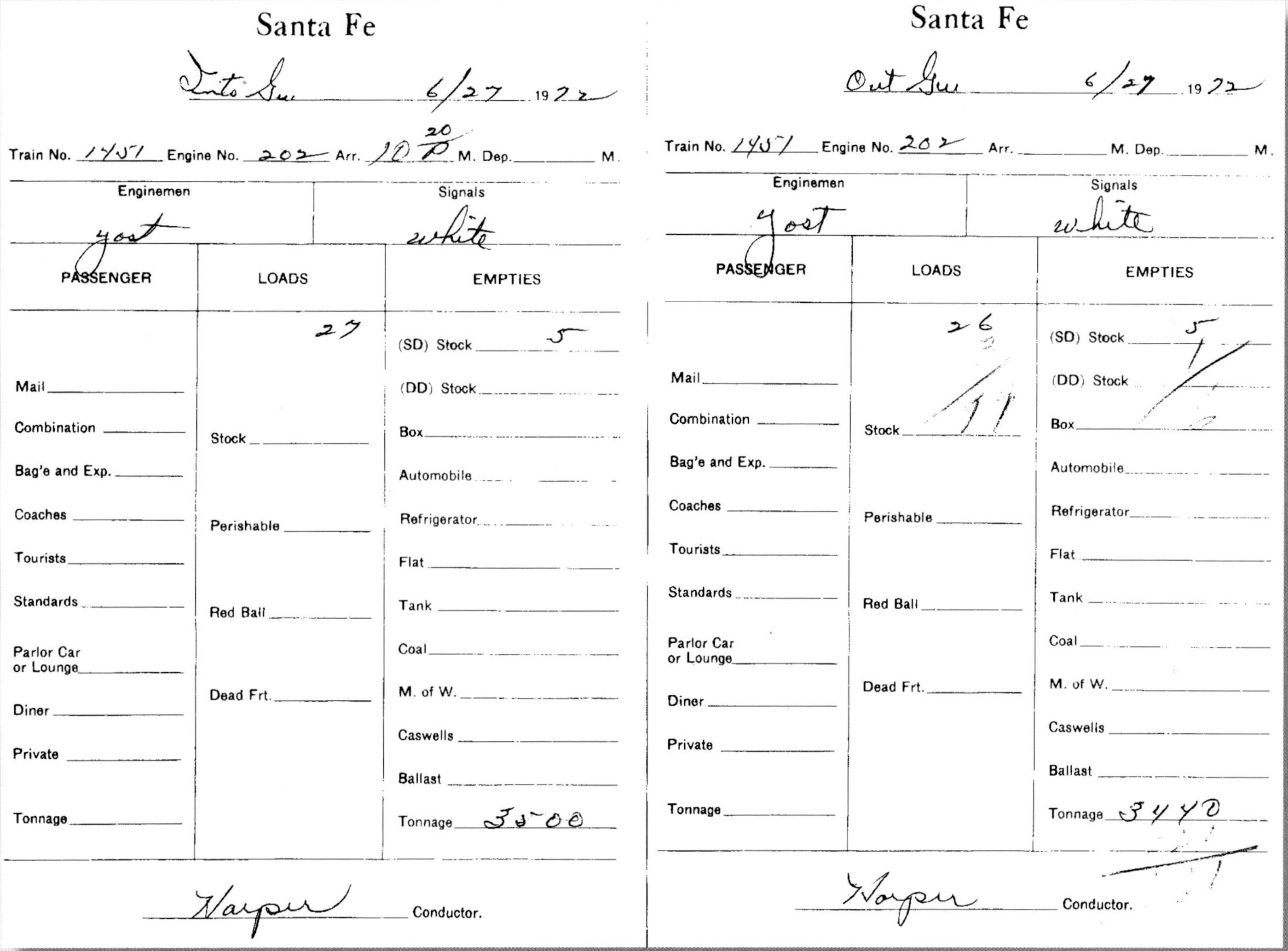

Santa Fe

Into Gu 6/27 1922

Train No. 1451 Engine No. 202 Arr. 10 20 P M. Dep. ______ M.

Enginemen	Signals
Yost	white

PASSENGER		LOADS		EMPTIES	
			27	(SD) Stock	5
Mail				(DD) Stock	
Combination		Stock		Box	
Bag'e and Exp.				Automobile	
Coaches		Perishable		Refrigerator	
Tourists				Flat	
Standards		Red Ball		Tank	
Parlor Car or Lounge				Coal	
Diner		Dead Frt.		M. of W.	
Private				Caswells	
				Ballast	
Tonnage				Tonnage	3500

Harper Conductor.

Santa Fe

Out Gu 6/27 1922

Train No. 1451 Engine No. 202 Arr. ______ M. Dep. ______ M.

Enginemen	Signals
Yost	white

PASSENGER		LOADS		EMPTIES	
			26	(SD) Stock	5
Mail				(DD) Stock	
Combination		Stock		Box	
Bag'e and Exp.				Automobile	
Coaches		Perishable		Refrigerator	
Tourists				Flat	
Standards		Red Ball		Tank	
Parlor Car or Lounge				Coal	
Diner		Dead Frt.		M. of W.	
Private				Caswells	
				Ballast	
Tonnage				Tonnage	3440

Harper Conductor.

Conductor's Order Sheet

Rock Island train c. 1940. Otto Perry photo from Denver Public Library.

Six
More Steam Railroads Come to Guthrie

The bustle of Oklahoma's first capital soon attracted more railroads eager to add revenues to their coffers. Chugging on the heels of each other came the likes of the **Chicago, Rock Island & Pacific** (1902), the **St. Louis & San Francisco** (1902), the **Fort Smith & Western** (1903), the **Missouri, Kansas & Texas** (1903), the **St. Louis, El Reno & Western,** (1903). Chapter seven will cover the electric lines, the **Guthrie Railway,** and the electric interurban **Oklahoma Railway Company.**

The Rock Island line's role in the Peavine railroad's operation was discussed earlier. The Rock Island obtained another access to Guthrie from the east. At this time, the Rock Island and the **Choctaw, Oklahoma & Gulf** were bitter competitive rivals. It appeared they would be duplicating lines unnecessarily. The remedy came when the Rock Island leased all the Choctaw lines in 1902. The Choctaw line (previously named the **Choctaw, Oklahoma & Western**) had original access to Guthrie that now passed to the Rock Island, allowing its allied Peavine Railroad to extend to Chandler.

EDMON LOW LIBRARY, OKLAHOMA STATE UNIVERSITY

1/23/1902	**Choctaw, Oklahoma and Gulf Railroad Company (CO&G #2) (Terr. of OK)**
	Incorporated "for the purpose of constructing, maintaining and operating a line of standard gauge railroad together with lines of telegraph and telephone and all other accessories or appurtenances now known to the art of building, constructing or operating railroads or which may hereafter be discovered or developed. Said line shall extend from and through the corporate limits of the City of Guthrie in Logan County, Oklahoma Territory in an easterly or southeasterly direction through the Counties of Logan and Lincoln to a connection with a line of railroad of the Choctaw, Oklahoma and Gulf Railroad Company in the Creek Nation, Indian Territory, an estimated length of sixty five miles, with the right to build a branch line from some point on said line of railroad in Lincoln County through said Lincoln County and Pottawatomie County to a connection with the present line of the Choctaw, Oklahoma and Gulf Railroad Company in said Pottawatomie County at or near the City of Shawnee, Oklahoma Territory, an estimated length of thirty (30) miles." Name changed to Choctaw, Oklahoma and Western Railroad Company on [5/5/1902].

5/5/1902	**Choctaw, Oklahoma and Western Railroad Company (?)**
	Patent amended authorizing the "constructing, maintaining and operating of a line of standard gauge railroad for the transportation of freight and passengers, together with lines of telegraph and telephone, and any and all other accessories or appurtenances now known to the art of building, constructing, or operating railroads, usually incident or convenient thereto, or which may hereafter be discovered or developed in connection therewith; and for the purpose of maintaining and operating such railroad, telegraph and telephone lines, together with side tracks, wyes, buildings and structures of any kind or character whatsoever convenient for the maintenance and operation thereof; and for the purpose generally of exercising any and all powers, rights, franchises, or privileges conferred upon such corporations by the laws of the Territory of Oklahoma and together with all the powers, rights, privileges and franchises conferred by, or to be exercised under the authority of any laws of the United States in the construction, maintenance or operation of such line of railroad and through any district, county, reservation, Indian Reservation, Indian Allotment or lands wholly or partially under the control or jurisdiction of the United States or the Territory of Oklahoma, and through the lands of any Indian Tribe or Nation or Allotted lands in Indian Territory or any lands held by Indian occupants, according to the laws, usages and customs of any Indian Tribe or Nation in Indian Territory, or in and through any municipality in Oklahoma Territory or in Indian Territory, together with the right, power and authority to lease or sell all or any part of its line or lines of railway to any other railroad company, or to consolidate all or any part of its line or lines of railway with any other railroad company."

Name changed from Choctaw, Oklahoma and Gulf Railroad Company (CO&G #2) [1/23/1902] on 5/5/1902

Built from Guthrie to Chandler, Oklahoma, (38 miles) via Bestin, Frost, Iconium, Merrick, Dudley, Emsey, Lowe and North Yard by ~1903.

Sold to Chicago, Rock Island and Pacific Railway Company (CRI&P #3) [6/2-3/1880] on 3/24/1904.

Evidently, the Rock Island line was involved with corporate maneuvering similar to the Santa Fe's acquisitions during this time period. The Rock Island served Guthrie until June 1, 1924. At that time, abandonment of the line between Guthrie and Chandler was approved. The freight depot is the only readily visible remnant of the Rock Island in Guthrie today. A few years back, a local group formed to rehabilitate the building and the building is now looking fine. The Rock Island Railroad ceased existence in 1980. As a so-called "Granger Road," it could not survive the Interstate Highway truck commerce or competition from the rival railroads. Some Rock Island routes were saved by private purchase while the State of Oklahoma preserved much of the old Choctaw route from Oklahoma City to near the Texas border. The **Union Pacific Railroad** acquired the eastern line from Oklahoma City. Sic Transit Gloria, old Rock Island Line.

The former Rock Island freight depot at Guthrie, Oklahoma in 1999 before the recent overhaul.

This photo illustrates the Rock Island yard at Kingfisher, Oklahoma, and grain elevators, c. 1906.

JOHN GILMOUR COLLECTION

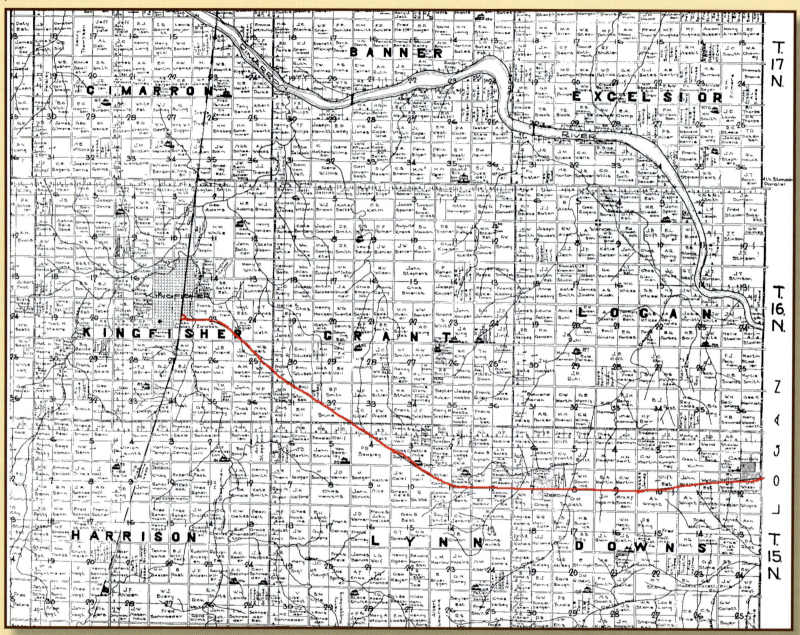

Map showing wye at Kingfisher and Peavine line to Cashion.

The **St. Louis & San Francisco Railroad (Frisco)** was the next line to venture into Guthrie. In fact, according to a letter sent to Santa Fe officials in Guthrie, the Eastern Oklahoma Railway Company surveying team encountered a rival team from the Frisco while scouting potential grades east of Guthrie in 1899. From maps, letters, oral reports and timetables, one is hard pressed to determine whether the Frisco ever laid track into Guthrie. More likely, they obtained trackage rights over the Rock Island line from Chandler to Guthrie. Since Chandler was a station on the Frisco Tulsa to Oklahoma City line, this was a logical choice. Early on, the Frisco cast its lot with Oklahoma City whose officials were maneuvering to move the state capital there from Guthrie. Since the Santa Fe was the dominant rail player in Guthrie, such a transfer would level the railroad playing yard, so to speak, in favor of the Frisco. In fact, the movement of the state capital was a nasty blow to the fortunes of Guthrie, for only recently has Guthrie revitalized itself after years of stagnation. If progressive leaders such as **George Watts** and others continue their efforts, Guthrie may yet become a showplace town, attractive to both tourists and residents. Its natural charm, location historic buildings, preservation district and vibrant art community are strong attractions that need more promotion..

The Frisco ceased operations into Guthrie in 1906, turning over all its traffic to the Rock Island. The Frisco was an aggressive, well run railroad. It survived until merged into the Burlington Northern system in 1980. It is ironic that the Frisco and Santa Fe, once bitter rivals, are now part of the BNSF Railroad. As Yogi Berra might say, it's *deja vue* all over again!

Cheap Rates
For the
Holidays.

December 20, 21, 22, 23, 24, 25, 30 and 31, 1906 and January; 7, 1907.
Tickets sold on these dates between all stations on Rock Island lines at special rates.

Fare and One-third
For the Round Trip

Minimum rate 25 cents. Tickets good to and Including January 7, 1907.
Talk with the Rock Island man about your trip

W. E. BENNETT
Enid, Okla.

Rock Island ad from Philip Moseley.

Common stock certificate, St. Louis & San Francisco Railway Company.

The 'Frisco' Steams into Guthrie

PHILIP MOSELEY COLLECTION

Frisco engine 4301 from Frisco web page.

FRISCO SYSTEM.

No. 450 Daily Lv		No. 451 Ar. Daily
5:15 p. m.	Guthrie	8:05 a. m.
7:11 p. m.	Chandler	6:05 a. m.
7:22 p. m.	Chandler	5:52 a. m.
7:30 p. m.	Kansas City	7:15 p. m.
3:10 a. m.	Monnett	10:40 p. m.
7:20 a. m.	Monnett	10:30 p. m.
4:33 a. m.	Springfield	9:15 p. m.
11:50 a. m.	St. Louis	2:30 p. m.
6:30 p. m.	Memphis	9:15 a. m.
6:40 a. m.	Birmingham	10:30 p. m.

MIXED—DAILY.

No. 452		No. 453
9:00 a. m.	Guthrie	9:00 p. m.
11:50 a. m.	Chandler	6:30 p. m.
12:05 p. m.	Chandler	6:15 p. m.
7:20 a. m.	Kansas City	11:30 p. m.
6:30 p. m.	Monnett	10:15 p. m.
6:50 p. m.	Monnett	10:00 p. m.
10:50 p. m.	Springfield	7:45 p. m.
7:55 a. m.	St. Louis	11:00 p. m.
6:00 a. m.	Memphis	8:35 p. m.
	Birmingham	12:30 p. m.

Frisco Guthrie timetable from 1902.

ST. LOUIS AND SAN FRANCISCO RAILROAD COMPANY.

PASSENGER TRAFFIC DEPARTMENT.

CIRCULAR No. 2984.

Line Between Chandler, O. T., and Guthrie, O. T., Operated by the Rock Island System.

SAINT LOUIS, December 1, 1905.

CONNECTING LINES:

The line of road between Chandler, O. T., and Guthrie, O. T., which was operated by this Company up to November 1, 1905, is now operated by the Chicago, Rock Island & Pacific Railway. Tickets to points between Chandler and Guthrie should now bear one coupon account St. Louis & San Francisco R. R. from its terminals to Chandler, and another coupon account Chicago, Rock Island & Pacific Ry. from Chandler to destination. Such form of ticket could also be used for business to stations on the C. R. I. & P. west of Guthrie.

Stations between Chandler and Guthrie affected by this arrangement are as follows:

LOWE, O. T.	ICONIUM, O. T.
DUDLEY, O. T.	TAYLOR, O. T.
MERRICK, O. T.	GUTHRIE, O. T.

Assistant General Passenger Agent.

General Passenger Agent.

Thanks to John B. Moore, Jr.

AUTHOR PHOTO

Frisco steam engine No. 1519 stands proudly at the Enid Railroad Museum in 1999. Originally, there was a plan to use this engine to haul dinner trains up to Enid. We can only hold hope for this.

A Frisco GP c. 1980.

Frisco E unit prior to merger with BN.

The next railroad to serve Guthrie was one that still makes some local old timers' eyes blink with tears: **The Fort Smith & Western Railroad Company**. It was incorporated under Arkansas law on January 25, 1899, to construct a line westerly from Ft. Smith, Arkansas, to a point in Lincoln County, east of Guthrie, Oklahoma. In 1903, the track was completed from that point to Guthrie. Later, to conserve time and expense, the FS&W (also known as "The Footsore and Weary") obtained trackage rights from the **Missouri-Kansas-Texas Railroad** over that line from Sparks, Oklahoma to Oklahoma City. The Eastern Oklahoma line of the Santa Fe crossed the FS&W at Fallis, also. The two roads shared station and yard facilities, there as well as at Guthrie.

The FS&W was another railroad built a "Hundred miles too long or a hundred years too soon." It served a territory of small towns and meager business. Surprisingly, Andrew Mellon, one of the great American financial moguls, was a director of this forlorn line. The woebegone **St. Louis, El Reno & Western**, a line that never came close to St. Louis or went west of El Reno was taken over by the FS&W in 1906 This be-knighted railroad was incorporated January 5, 1903 in Oklahoma Territory and started operations in June 1904 after 42.2 miles of track were laid between Guthrie and El Reno through Navina.

The FS&W acquired fifty-one percent of the stock of the El Reno & Western in 1906. Receivers were appointed in 1915 and the road was abandoned and track dismantled in 1924. One interesting feature was use of a 0-4-4T engine, No. 21 on this line. In 1926, **The Oklahoma Railway Company** purchased the terminal property in El Reno and operated over the tracks there until it was abandoned. The Footsore and Weary itself was abandoned in 1939. Some traces of the old grade and parts of the Guthrie wye can still be explored today.

FRISCO WEB PAGE

Frisco engine No. 4519 is ready to roll.

USDA PHOTO

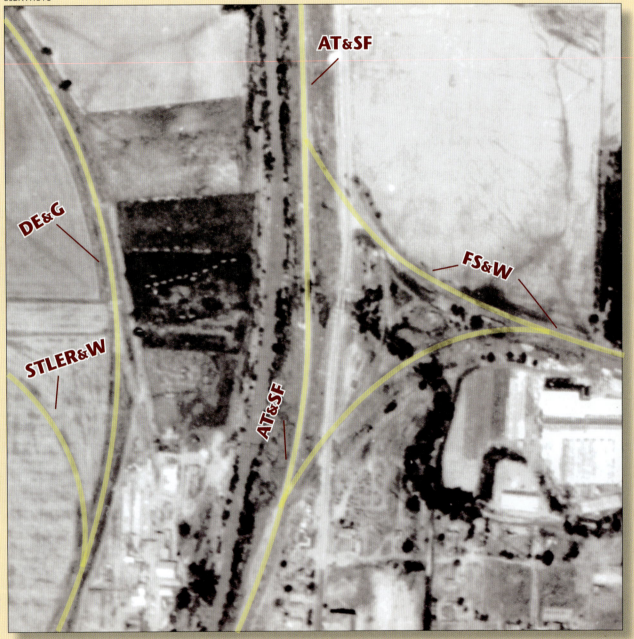

An aerial photo of the Fort Smith & Western wye just north of Guthrie depot taken in 1938. The FS&W comes in from the right and joins the Santa Fe main line in the middle of the frame. On the lower left, one can see the DE&G line with the St. Louis, El Reno & Western track turning west from that line.

All aboard the FS&W

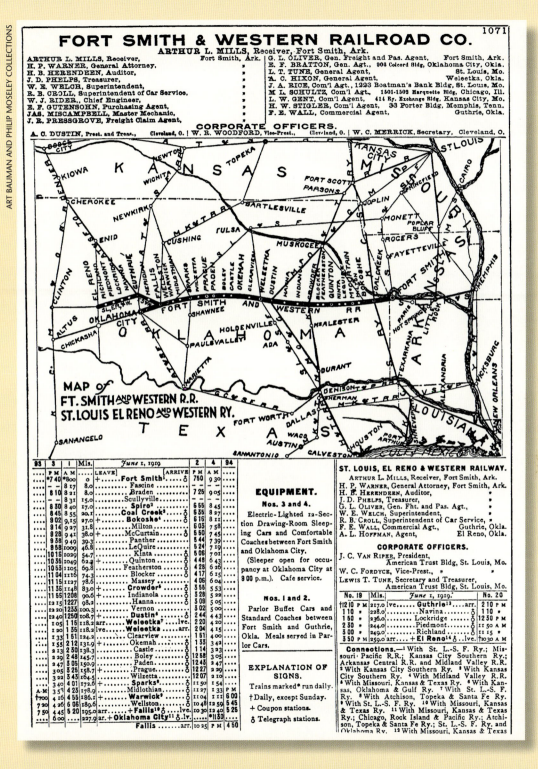

PLATE 115. Ft. Smith & Western 4-6-0 1st No. 10, photographed in Guthrie, Oklahoma. (*Courtesy John B. Fink Collection Division of Manuscripts, University of Oklahoma*)

Fort Smith & Western engine No. 4 with passenger train ready to depart Guthrie, Oklahoma, c. 1904

ART BAUMAN COLLECTION

ART BAUMAN COLLECTION

FS&W engine No. 11 somewhere in Oklahoma.

ART BAUMAN COLLECTION

FS&W caboose at Guthrie, c. 1938.

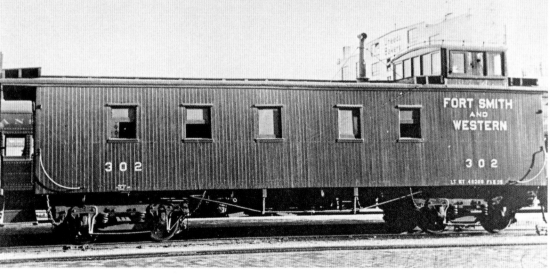

FS&W/AT&SF interchange, Sparks, Oklahoma, date unknown, and map below from Art Bauman collection.

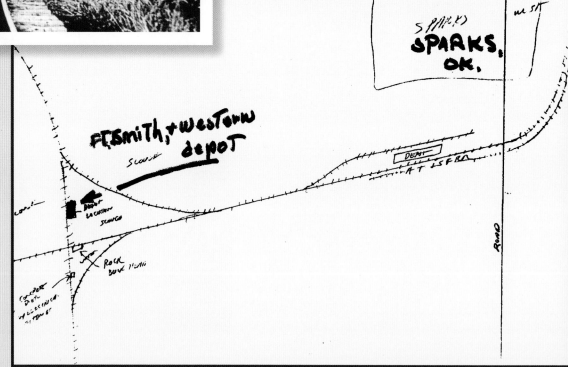

FS&W depot at Sparks, Oklahoma, date unknown.

FS&W track gang near El Reno, Oklahoma. Date unknown.

JOHN GILMOUR COLLECTION

St. Louis, El Reno & Western engine #21, a 0-4-4T type at El Reno, Oklahoma, date unknown.

AUTHOR COLLECTION

FS&W engine No. 1 at El Reno, Oklahoma, c. 1902.

MKT Alco diesel No 142 c. 1985.

The **Missouri, Kansas and Oklahoma Railway** steamed into Guthrie hot on the wheels of the FS&W. It was incorporated in Oklahoma Territory in 1903 and laid 23.0 miles of track between Fallis and Guthrie. All the assets of the MK&O were taken over by the parent **Missouri, Kansas and Texas (MKT or Katy)** in 1904. The Katy operated in Guthrie only 15 years counting the MK&O period. The Katy abandoned operations in Guthrie in November 1918.

The railroad operated trains from Sedalia, Missouri through Cushing, Oklahoma until this line was abandoned in the mid 1980s. The MKT was taken over by the **Union Pacific Railroad**'s subsidiary, **Missouri Pacific** in 1989. Currently, the Katy Historical Society publishes a quarterly magazine, *The Katy Flyer* and hosts an annual convention to preserve memories of the MKT.

MKT WEB PAGE

Missouri-Kansas-Texas Railroad - Wikipedia, the free encyclopedia

Missouri-Kansas-Texas Railroad

From Wikipedia, the free encyclopedia

*For other meanings of **MKT** see MKT (disambiguation)*

The **Missouri-Kansas-Texas Railroad** (known as the **MKT**, or **Katy**) began as the Union Pacific Railway, Southern Branch (unrelated to the Union Pacific Railroad) in 1865. It was the first railroad to enter Texas from the north. In 1896 the Katy crashed two locomotives as a publicity stunt.

Eventually the Katy's core system would grow to link Kansas City and St. Louis, Missouri; Tulsa and Oklahoma City, Oklahoma; Dallas, Fort Worth, Waco, Temple, Austin, San Antonio, Houston, and Galveston, Texas. An additional mainline between Fort Worth and Salina, Kansas was added in the 1980s after the collapse of the Rock Island Railroad; this line was operated as the Oklahoma, Kansas and Texas Railroad (OKKT).

Missouri-Kansas-Texas Railroad

Reporting marks	MKT
Locale	Kansas, Missouri, Oklahoma, and Texas
Dates of operation	1865 – 1989
Successor line	Missouri Pacific
Track gauge	4 ft 8½ in (1435 mm) (standard gauge)
Headquarters	Dallas, Texas

The Katy's purchase by the Missouri Pacific Railroad Company (MoPac) and the MoPac's owner, the Union Pacific, was approved in 1988. The M-K-T is now part of the Union Pacific Railroad system. On December 1, 1989, the Katy was formally merged into the MoPac. A large portion of the Missouri track has been converted into a Missouri State Park: the Katy Trail. A 3.5 mi (6 km) long section is being converted into a multi-use trail through downtown Dallas, linking White Rock lake to the American Airlines Center.

The former M-K-T rail line (20 miles) which linked Katy to Downtown Houston has been converted; a section between Loop 610 and Katy, TX is part of the Interstate 10 expansion since TxDOT purchased the M-K-T right-of-way in 1998, and the M-K-T line east of Loop 610 into Downtown Houston is currently owned by the City of Houston's Parks and Recreation Department (plans are underway to convert the right-of-way into a bicycle trail).

The large and attractive Houston suburb of Katy, Texas, is named after the railroad's nickname. A blues song, "She Caught the Katy" - written by Taj Mahal and Yank Rachell - makes mention of the MKT. The song was prominently featured in the 1980 movie *The Blues Brothers*. Folk-rocker Gillian Welch references the lyrics to "She Caught the Katy" in her 2001 song, "Revelator", the title track on her Time (The Revelator) album.

In July 2005, Union Pacific unveiled a brand new EMD SD70ACe locomotive, Union Pacific 1988, in MKT colors as part of a new heritage program.

An interesting Wikipedia article on the history of the Missouri-Kansas-Texas Railroad.

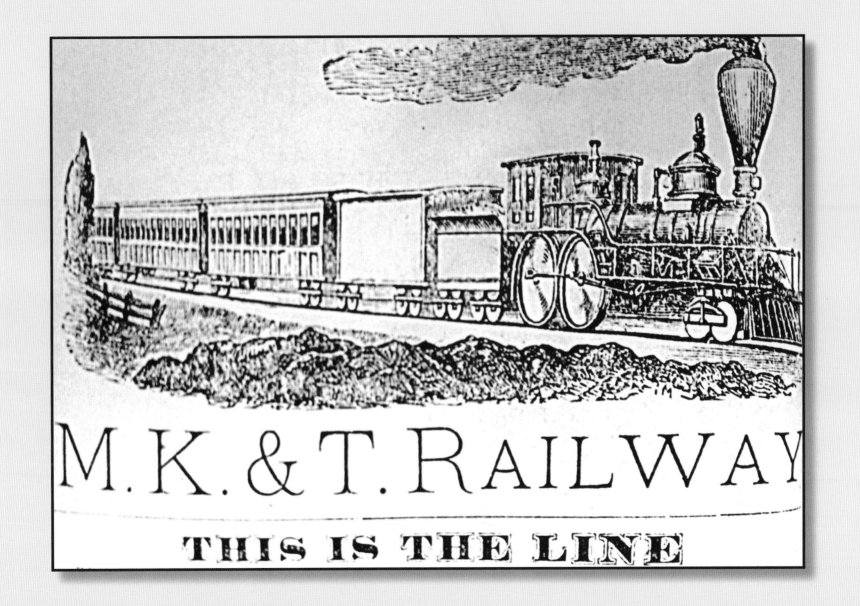

PHILIP MOSELEY PHOTO

The former Katy/Rock Island yard at Guthrie, Oklahoma in 2006.

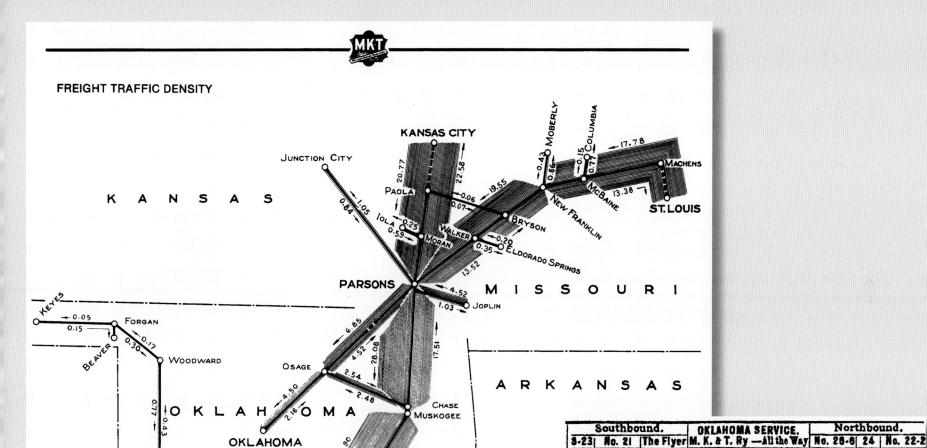

Both illustrations above courtesy of Jerry Pitts and Katy Railway Historical Society.

THANKS TO GORDON NEFF AND PHIL MORROW.

Subj: **MK&T TT Schedule OKC to Guthrie**
Date: 6/14/2006 6:05:47 A.M. Pacific Standard Time
From: JJPi
To: JCamma455

Hello Joe,

The earliest MK&T TT I have in my collection is dated September 1, 1908.

It shows note stating: Guthrie passengers change cars at Fallis.

The southbound Katy Flyer left Fallis at 3:57 PM and arrived at OKC at 5:20 PM.

Guthrie passengers arrived at Guthrie at 5:10 PM.

Northbound Katy Flyer left OKC at 10:40 AM and arrived at Fallis at 11:57 AM.

Guthrie passengers left Guthrie at 10:45 AM for Fallis.

Train 21 southbound left Fallis at 8:58 AM and arrived at Guthrie at 10:05 AM.

Train 21 arrived at OKC at 10:15 AM.

Northbound Train 22 left OKC at 7:00 PM for Fallis. Train 22 left Fallis at 7:45 PM.

Guthrie passengers left Guthrie at 6:25 PM for Fallis.

There was a Guthrie Division of the MK&T in 1908 with four daily southbound trains No.565, 109, 107, and 105. Northbound counterparts were the No. 566, 110, 108, and 106. Stops between Fallis and Guthrie included Shiloh and Meridian. Trains 109, 105, 110, and 106 show departure and arrival times at Parsons, where Trains 565, 566, 107, and 108 do not.

It may be hard to get a clear copy of the actual TTs. The pages are yellow with age and the print size is quite small. I will experiment with enlarging the images and see what I can e-mail you. Give me a few days or so.

Jerry Pitts

Jerry Pitts wrote the author, furnishing this information.

LOGAN COUNTY HISTORY

For the Week of February 22-28

Sponsored by:

FIRST CAPITAL BANK

— 100 YEARS AGO —

IN 1903
- The Katy Railroad initiates two passenger trains a day between Guthrie and Fallis.
- The Ladies Auxiliary of the National Association of Mexican War Veterans asks congress to increase veterans pensions to $1 a day.

Guthrie Daily Ledger.

BRANCH LINE TRAINS

*Daily. †Daily, Except Sunday. xStops for Meals.
TRAINS DO NOT STOP WHERE NO TIME IS SHOWN.

Thanks to Jerry Pitts and Philip Moseley.

Track being laid for trolley line in Guthrie.

Seven
The Electric Lines of Guthrie

Guthrie was served for many years by a trolley line, the **Guthrie Street Railway**, and the interurban **Oklahoma Railway Company**. The clipping below recounts the rocky startup and ultimate quarter century success of Guthrie's downtown streetcars, which finally gave way to the automobile in 1929.

Guthrie Street Railway

Before Guthrie was a year old, civic leaders were looking towards a system of street railways. It was not until May 26, 1905, however, that a street railway system came into operation for the city.

June 8, 1889 the Council of East Guthrie granted a franchise, by ordinance, to J. H. Hamilton of Hamilton-Rankin Hardware Co. to operate an electric railway system in the city.

The company's deposit of $1000 to show good faith was eventually forfeited, amid considerable controversy. The city treasurer, Guy G. Farwell, drew the deposit from the Merchants Bank, placing it to the city's credit, only two days before the company attempted to stop payment.

Nothing further was done on obtaining a street railway until June 30, 1903, when John W. Shartel and A. H. Classen, of Oklahoma City, and a consortium, negotiated a franchise with the city for a proposed line of six miles of track.

Several delays were encountered, but eventually the line was built and opened with the 1905 celebration. The line, as dedicated that day, was described as starting at Drexel and Warner, west to Oak Street, 3 blocks south to Oklahoma, then west on Oklahoma to Seventh Street, north on Seventh to Warner, west on Warner to Fourteenth, then south to the terminal on Cleveland. Another route started on the corner of Drexel and Springer, west on Springer to Ash, north to Harrison, west to Second, then north to Oklahoma. The Harrison Ave. and Oklahoma Ave. lines connected at Division, and made a loop around the two blocks west of Division, between Harrison and Oklahoma. An extra line was laid on Harrison from Division east to Vine, making a double track capable of handling the crowds that would exit from Brooks Opera House.

Immediately after the main line was operative, the company, known as the Guthrie Railway Co., began work on a line southward to Mineral Wells (Island) Park and the new ball park area, also known as Electric Park. The line crossed Snake Creek on a piling bridge.

The streetcars met with enthusiastic support from the public, providing economical and convenient transportation within the city at the time. Usage declined, however, with the coming of automobiles, and by 1929, the service was no longer operating.

Some of the tracks had been removed, primarily those on unpaved streets. The Guthrie City Council faced the problem of removal of the remaining tracks and repair of the streets, holding that the railway company was responsible for removal of the tracks. This started a long period of litigation, with the tracks remaining. They were eventually covered over when the city resurfaced streets in the last half of the 1950s.

GUTHRIE TERRITORIAL MUSEUM ARCHIVES.

Guthrie streetcar inspection trip, C. 1905.

Guthrie Railway spike ceremony, December 9, 1905.

A Guthrie Railway car on Harrison Street.

Guthrie Railway cars on Main Street.

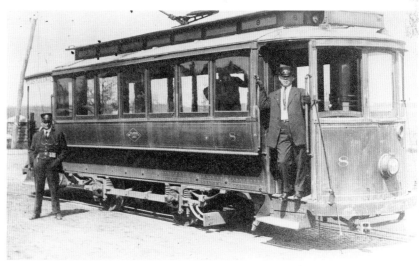

Guthrie streetcar on Harrison Street.

The interurban **Oklahoma Railway Company** incorporated on June 14, 1904 as the **Oklahoma City Railway**. The name was changed to Oklahoma Railway Company in 1907. The company acquired a perpetual charter under territorial laws to incorporate, own, buy and acquire electric street railways and lighting plants. The line was started in 1903, ran to Yukon in 1909, then north from Edmond to Guthrie in 1916, building 16.0 miles of track for that segment. The tracks ran a little distance from the Santa Fe main line. The construction of public highways and use of the private automobile cut into the Oklahoma Railway's traffic loads. However, the interurban line enjoyed a brief period of prosperity during World War II when restricted auto use forced mass use of rail passenger transport. Also, the U.S. Navy had a base in Norman, Oklahoma and the sailors patronized the line running from there to Oklahoma City. The electric line ceased operations in 1946. Some tracks may still be seen in contemporary Guthrie near the depot.

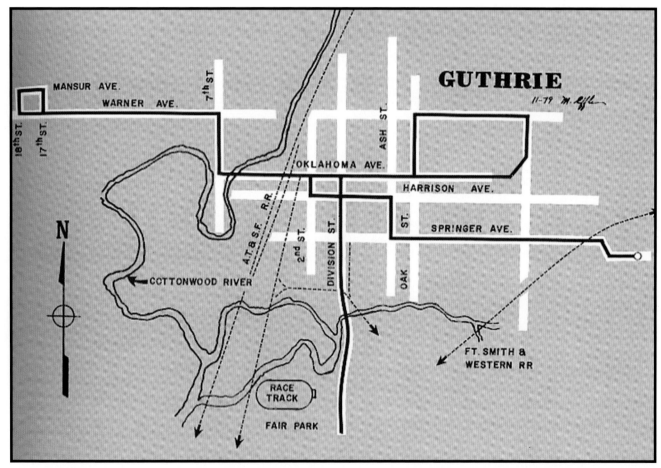

Guthrie Railway Map.

AUTHOR COLLECTION

PRESTON GEORGE COLLECTION

Preston George shot this Oklahoma Railway trolley in Guthrie.

PRESTON GEORGE COLLECTION

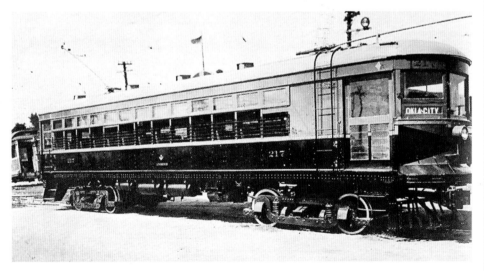

Preston George caught this larger car in Guthrie.

AUTHOR COLLECTION

A remnant of Oklahoma Railway track in 1999 Guthrie. The depot is in the right background.

EVAN STAIR PHOTO

Amtrak delivers: *The Heartland Flyer* visits Guthrie on September 30, 2006 after a 27-year hiatus.

Eight
Guthrie—Always on Amtrak?

The Santa Fe terminated its rail passenger business on May 1, 1971, along with almost all other American passenger railroads. At that time, **Amtrak,** a government agency, assumed responsibility for running all passenger trains except for those of the **Denver & Rio Grande Western**, **Rock Island** and **Southern Railway**. Under Amtrak, the Chicago to Houston/Galveston *Texas Chief* continued to run through Oklahoma, with stops at Guthrie and Oklahoma City. Several years later, due to pressure from the image-unhappy Santa Fe, Amtrak renamed the train as the *Lone Star*. Amtrak discontinued this train on October 10, 1979. Thus, from this date, Oklahoma did not have interstate rail passenger service until the year 2001-initiation of the *Heartland Flyer*, traveling a daily roundtrip from Oklahoma City to Fort Worth, Texas. So Guthrie had no rail passenger service from 1979 until the three-day runs of the *Heartland Flyer* in 2006.

Thus, in 2001, thanks to local initiative, Amtrak did initiate the *Heartland Flyer*, one that has become a well patronized train due to the hard work and persistence of Oklahomans such as *Passenger Rail Oklahoma* members **Evan Stair, Michelle Brown, Karl Rambo, Nelson Dent, and John Woodard**. In 2006 these dedicated advocates joined forces with Guthrie citizens **Philip Moseley, Gordon Neff, Artie Wangler**, City Manager **Glen Hays**, and Chamber of Commerce president **Kathy Montgomery** to persuade Amtrak to extend the *Heartland Flyer* to Guthrie to serve travelers coming to a late-summer festival. They were successful. Amtrak extended the run north from Oklahoma City to terminate in Guthrie to accommodate this event. The Guthrie train ran three days, September 30, October 1 and October 2 and was used well, according to reports. Joining in the communal spirit, I called Amtrak reservations and bought a ticket to support the cause despite being unable to be on site to ride the train.

Currently, these citizens are lobbying Amtrak and the Oklahoma Department of Transportation to extend the *Heartland Flyer* to Newton, Kansas to meet the *Southwest Chief,* a long distance train that travels between Chicago and Los Angeles in both directions daily. Also, there is additional movement to restore Amtrak service between Tulsa and Oklahoma City. Time will tell if factors such as the oil crisis, environmental concerns and increasing road infrastructure damage from heavy trucks will impact personal and government economies sufficiently to enhance the feasibility of expanding all rail services. We know that the rail mode is more efficient in energy consumption and ability to move large cargos and numbers of passengers vis-a-vis other modes of transportation.

JOHN FINK PHOTO FROM JOHN B. MOORE, JR.

Doodlebug M179 is ready to leave Guthrie for Enid and Kiowa, c. 1946.

Evan Stair sent this photo of a Frisco passenger train arriving at Pawnee, Oklahoma, c.1905.

Santa Fe Meal Service
Fred Harvey

The dining-room, lunch-room, dining-car, and station-hotel service of the Santa Fe is managed by Fred Harvey. It is a service unequaled in American railroading. It sets the standard. On the Santa Fe you do not eat in an eating-house; you dine at a dining station. There's a difference—the Fred Harvey "difference."

The Fred Harvey organization has more than 4,000 employes, trained with the "desire to please." Besides other activities, approximately 12,000,000 meals were served at the various dining stations during the year 1924.

Few of the perishable foodstuffs are bought in the open market. Trained men go into the most noted orchards looking for the choicest fruits. There is a department composed of experts who know all about meat. The poultry is milk-fed on Harvey chicken farms. Collection centers are established for the advantageous purchase of eggs. The purity of milk and cream is assured by Harvey dairy farms.

Recently, large sums of money have been spent by the Santa Fe in expanding and improving many of the dining stations. The capacity of the lunch rooms has been doubled or trebled. This enlargement of facilities is necessary to meet the heavy demand caused by increased travel. At whatever cost the standard must be maintained.

All through passenger trains, which do not carry dining cars, are scheduled to stop at dining stations placed at convenient points along the line, and indicated in time tables thus —●. Ample time is allowed for meals.

Dining-room meals for trains en route are served table d'hote price, $1.00 for adults, and 75 cents for children occupying seats at table. Service at Chicago, El Paso, Galveston, Houston, Kansas City, Lamy, Wichita and Williams is a la carte.

Lunch-room meals are served a la carte; prices reasonable

Dining-car meals are served a la carte, except that dinner on trains Nos. 3 and 4 (The California Limited) is table d'hote, $1.50.

The dining rooms are located at intervals of about 100 miles, to meet the emergencies of train operation. They present an attractive appearance, the environment being like that of a club. Experienced travelers like to get off the train at meal time for a few minutes' exercise in the open air.

The dining rooms at Emporia, Hutchinson, Syracuse, Wellington, Temple, Trinidad, Las Vegas, Albuquerque, Clovis, Williams, Ash Fork and Needles are in the Harvey hotels, adjacent to the station. Those at other points are located in the Santa Fe station, except that the restaurant at Chicago is in Dearborn Station; at Kansas City, in Union Station; at Wichita, Kan., in Union Station; at El Paso, Tex., in Union Depot, and at Houston, Tex., in Union Station, and in Galveston, Tex., in Union Station.

Meals a la carte served on Santa Fe ferries between San Francisco and Ferry Point.

The lunch rooms admirably care for those who only wish a light meal. The utmost care is exercised as to quality of food and its preparation.

DINING ROOMS — SEATING CAPACITY

Albuquerque, N.M. 127	Dodge City, Kan. 118	Purcell, Okla. 54
Amarillo, Tex. 70	El Paso, Tex. 100	San Bernardino, Cal. 100
Arkansas City, Kan. 72	Emporia, Kan. 104	Seligman, Ariz. 80
Ash Fork, Ariz. 120	Ft. Worth, Tex. 24	Somerville, Tex. 10
Bakersfield, Cal. 72	Gallup, N.M. 112	Syracuse, Kan. 104
Barstow, Cal. 110	Grand Canyon, Ariz. 150	Temple, Tex. 68
Belen, N.M. 64	Hutchinson, Kan. 110	Topeka, Kan. 60
Brownwood, Tex. 62	Kansas City, Mo. 150	Trinidad, Colo. 104
Canadian, Tex.*	Kingman, Ariz.*	Vaughn, N.M. 80
Chanute, Kan.*	La Junta, Colo. 200	Waynoka, Okla. 56
Chicago, Ill. (Dearborn Sta.) 79	Lamy, N.M. 9	Wellington, Kan. 72
Clovis, N.M. 82	Las Vegas, N.M. 108	Wichita, Kan. 44
Colorado Spgs., Colo. 60	Needles, Cal. 152	Williams, Ariz. 70
	Newton, Kan.	Winslow, Ariz. 124

*Temporarily closed.

LUNCH ROOMS — SEATING CAPACITY

Albuquerque, N.M. 113	Ft. Worth, Tex. 38	Rincon, N.M. 31
Amarillo, Tex. 38	Gainesville, Tex. 42	San Bernardino, Cal. 69
Arkansas City, Kan. 30	Gallup, N.M. 81	San Diego, Cal. 41
Ash Fork, Ariz. 62	Galveston, Tex. 74	San Marcial, N.M. 24
Bakersfield, Cal. 47	Grand Canyon, Ariz. 120	Seligman, Ariz. 47
Barstow, Cal. 52	Guthrie, Okla. 34	Slaton, Tex. 46
Belen, N.M. 48	Houston, Tex. 91	Somerville, Tex. 46
Brownwood, Tex. 33	Hutchinson, Kan. 48	Sweetwater, Tex. 35
Canadian, Tex. 38	Kansas City, Mo. 250	Syracuse, Kan. 51
Chanute, Kan. 31	Kingman, Ariz. 42	Temple, Tex. 20
Chicago, Ill. (Dearborn Sta.) 34	La Junta, Colo. 64	Trinidad, Colo. 28
Cleburne, Tex. 42	Lamy, N.M. 34	Vaughn, N.M. 42
Clovis, N.M. 42	Las Vegas, N.M. 51	Waynoka, Okla. 37
Colorado Spgs., Colo. 47	Los Angeles, Cal. 48	Wellington, Kan. 31
Deming, N.M. 46	Mojave, Cal. 56	Wichita, Kan. 33
Dodge City, Kan. 47	Needles, Cal. 104	Williams, Ariz. 53
El Paso, Tex. 42	Newton, Kan. 35	Winslow, Ariz. 72
Emporia, Kan. 44	Purcell, Okla. 22	

The station hotels along the Santa Fe are conveniently located for business and sightseeing. Hotel accommodations are provided at

GUEST ROOMS

Albuquerque, N.M. 121	Hutchinson, Kan. 79	Somerville, Tex. 5
Ash Fork, Ariz. 22	La Junta, Colo. 40	Sweetwater, Tex. 10
Barstow, Cal. 28	Lamy, N.M. 8	Syracuse, Kan. 15
Clovis, N.M. 22	Las Vegas, N.M. 37	Temple, Tex. 23
Dodge City, Kan. 46	Needles, Cal. 25	Trinidad, Colo. 20
Emporia, Kan. 7	Newton, Kan. 39	Vaughn, N.M. 5
Gallup, N.M. 68	Rincon, N.M. 14	Wellington, Kan. 8
Grand Canyon, Ariz. 91	San Marcial, N.M. 10	Williams, Ariz. 39
	Seligman, Ariz. 19	Winslow, Ariz. 12

At those hotels operated on the European plan the rates for rooms generally are $2.00 a day and upwards. Those operated on the American plan are $5.00 a day and upwards, except at the El Tovar, where the rate is $7.00 a day and upwards.

The most noteworthy of the Santa Fe hotels are:

	CAPACITY OF DINING ROOMS	NUMBER OF GUEST ROOMS	
THE BISONTE, at Hutchinson, Kan.	110	79	E
EL VAQUERO, at Dodge City, Kan.	118	46	A
THE SEQUOYAH, at Syracuse, Kan.	104	15	E
THE GRAN QUIVIRA, at Clovis, N.M.	82	22	E
THE CARDENAS, at Trinidad, Colo.	104	20	E
THE CASTAÑEDA, at Las Vegas, N.M.	108	37	E
EL ORTIZ, at Lamy, N.M.	9	8	E
THE ALVARADO, at Albuquerque, N.M.	127	121	A & E
EL NAVAJO, at Gallup, N.M.	112	68	E
THE FRAY MARCOS, at Williams, Ariz.	70	39	E
EL TOVAR, at Grand Canyon, Ariz.	150	91	A
THE ESCALANTE, at Ash Fork, Ariz.	120	22	E
EL GARCES, at Needles, Cal.	152	25	E
THE CASA DEL DESIERTO, at Barstow, Cal.	110	28	E

E—European Plan. A—American Plan.

The other rail-related issue impacting Guthrie is the current state of the former DE&G (Santa Fe Enid District) line connecting Guthrie with Fairmont. It may be in the best interests of Guthrie and the state of Oklahoma to evaluate potential revenue generation from freight traffic and excursion passenger trains running over this line. The right-of-way and bridges need repair, but the rails are heavy welded steel. All this effort will put people to work. On-going maintenance and other related activities could keep a number of Guthrie area people gainfully employed.

Both Oklahoma and Guthrie can benefit from increased tourism revenues. The 2007 celebration of the Centennial year of Oklahoma Statehood should attract significant numbers of visitors. The citizens of Guthrie should ponder this well. Guthrie is an attractive city with numerous historical and architectural attractions. These features can be made available more easily if convenient passenger train service was provided. Evan Stair and the other *Passenger Rail Oklahoma* advocates help keep this concept alive. Hail Guthrie!

Philip Moseley sent this list of Harvey House restaurants at Santa Fe depots.

EVAN STAIR PHOTO

Yost and Moseley are ready to depart Guthrie along with many other happy passengers.

COURTESY PHILIP MOSELEY

Steam is gone! Yard switcher is ready to go!

COURTESY PHILIP MOSELEY

Front view of the 627 Diesel Yard Switcher at Guthrie in 1957.

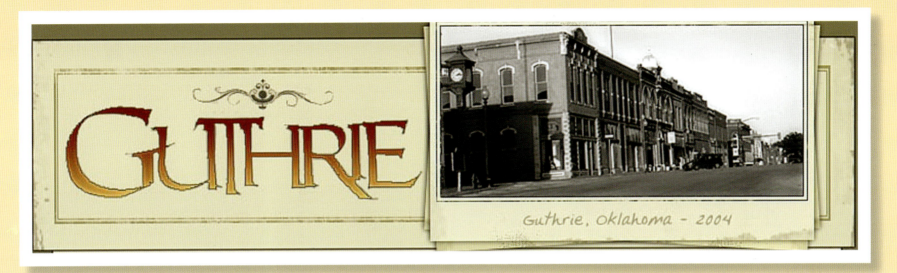

Guthrie, Oklahoma – 2004

In December 2006, Guthrie was voted "Favorite Small City" in a Daily Oklahoman newspaper poll.

Evan Stair, December 12, 2006.

Postcard showing the Hotel Ione, Guthrie.

Arkansas City, January 1, 1935.

All Concerned:

Offices on the Oklahoma Division will be open the hours indicated below, effective January 6, 1935:

Station	Weekdays	Sundays
"Dx"Arkansas Cy	Continuous	Continuous
Chilocco	7:30 AM to 4:30 PM	
Newkirk Tower	Continuous	Continuous
Ponca City	Continuous	Continuous
Marland	8:00 AM to 5:00 PM	8:00 AM to 10:00 AM
Red Rock	8:00 AM to 5:00 PM	8:15 AM to 10:15 AM
Perry	Continuous	4:45 AM to Midnight
Orlando	7:20 AM to 4:20 PM	
Mulhall	7:00 AM to 4:00 PM	
Guthrie	Continuous	Continuous
Edmond	6:15 AM to 10:40 PM	6:15 AM to 8:15 AM 12:00 N to 2:00 PM 4:00 PM to 6:00 PM 8:40 PM to 10:40 PM
Nowers (phone)	12:00 N to 9:00 PM	
Oklahoma Cy	Continuous	Continuous
Moore	8:00 AM to 5:00 PM	8:00 AM to 1:00 PM
Norman	Continuous	Midnight to 3:30 AM 8:00 AM to 1:00 PM 5:00 PM to 9:30 PM
Noble	8:00 AM to 5:00 PM	
Purcell	Continuous	Continuous
Kaw	8:00 AM to 5:00 PM	1:50 PM to 3:50 PM
Burbank	8:00 AM to 5:00 PM	1:30 PM to 3:30 PM
DeNoya	8:00 AM to 5:00 PM	
Fairfax	8:00 AM to 7:00 PM	1:30 PM to 3:30 PM
Ralston	Continuous	6:00 AM to 8:00 AM 9:00 AM to 11:00 AM 1:30 PM to 3:30 PM
Skedee	8:00 AM to 5:00 PM	1:00 PM to 3:00 PM
Maramec	8:00 AM to 5:00 PM	
Yale	8:00 AM to 5:00 PM	
Cushing	Continuous	12:00 PM to 2:00 AM 8:00 AM to 12:05 PM 6:00 PM to 8:00 PM
Davenport	8:00 AM to 5:00 PM	
Sparks	8:15 AM to 5:15 PM	9:00 AM to 11:15 AM
Meeker	8:00 AM to 5:00 PM	9:15 AM to 11:15 AM
Shawnee Depot	6:45 AM to 3:45 PM	9:00 AM to 11:00 AM
So. Shawnee	7:00 AM to 11:00 PM	9:30 AM to 11:30 AM 3:00 PM to 6:00 PM

Station	Weekdays	Sundays
Pawnee	6:30 AM to 3:30 PM	6:30 AM to 8:30 AM
Glencoe	7:20 AM to 4:30 PM	
Stillwater	7:30 AM to 4:30 PM	7:30 AM to 9:30 AM
Ripley	7:30 AM to 4:30 PM	12:00 Noon to 2:00PM
Perkins	8:00 AM to 5:00 PM	
Coyle	8:00 AM to 5:00 PM	
Burlington	7:00 AM to 4:00 PM	
Cherokee	6:30 AM to 3:30 PM	6:30 AM to 9:30 AM
Jet	6:15 AM to 3:15 PM	
Nash	6:00 AM to 3:00 PM	
Hillsdale	6:00 AM to 3:00 PM	
Enid	9:00 AM to 6:00 PM	9:45 AM to 11:45 AM
Douglas	7:00 AM to 4:00 PM	
Marshall	6:00 AM to 3:00 PM	
Lovell	8:00 AM to 5:00 PM	
Crescent	7:00 AM to 4:00 PM	10:15 AM to 12:15 PM
Washington	8:00 AM to 5:00 PM	
Blanchard	8:00 AM to 5:00 PM	
Chickasha	8:00 AM to 5:00 PM	
Oilton	7:00 AM to 4:00 PM	
Drumright	8:30 AM to 5:30 PM	

At one man stations there will be one hour meal period between 11:30 AM and 1:30 PM.

Santa Fe Railway Agency Operating Hours on the Oklahoma Division.

Nine
More Guthrie Stories

Preston George and **Sylvan Wood** authored a definitive work, *The Railroads of Oklahoma*, in a 1943 quarterly published by the Railway & Locomotive Historical Society. George and Wood assembled an encyclopedic report, furnishing a marvelous reference vehicle for anyone interested in Oklahoma railroads. Several interesting stories are imbedded in this historical work.

It seems that John Rain, a Santa Fe engineer from 1881 to 1936, was driving a northbound train pulled by a small Hinkley consolidated (2-8-0) engine No. 228, on the Santa Fe Oklahoma Division main line just north of Guthrie. The water gave out about a mile from the Mulhall water tank and the crew was forced to extinguish the fire to avoid a boiler explosion. The crew uncoupled the engine and tried to pull it to the water tank using a pinch bar. Two cowboys rode up and watched the struggles with interest. They offered assistance that was readily accepted. The 'pokes looped lassos around both ends of the pilot beam and their ponies pulled the engine up to the tank. Engineer Rain was later to boast: "I'll bet I am the only engineer who ever got pulled to a water tank by a pair of cow ponies." Rain experienced another hairy adventure when the train he was driving was held up near Guthrie by the infamous outlaw, Al Jennings. Jennings boarded the train and held Mr. Rain under a huge gun muzzle while the train was looted by his fellow outlaws. In a stunning move, Jennings later turned straight and went to Hollywood to act in movies!

Another Santa Fe tale, perhaps apocryphal, involved engineer Haas piloting a southbound night passenger train just south of Guthrie. Coming around a slight curve, the driver spotted a brilliant white light over the tracks close ahead. He slammed the train into emergency to avoid a collision. To Haas' chagrin, it was soon revealed that the full moon was the culprit. The unwritten story-ending comment is that the engineer barely stopped in time….

Amtrak arrives in Guthrie. No moon available!

EVAN STAIR PHOTO

AT&SF engineer seniority list, July 1, 1948. Note familiar names, Nix, Slater and Griswold.

OKLAHOMA DIVISION
ROAD ENGINEERS SENIORITY ROSTER

#	Name	Date	#	Name	Date
1	Burns, Wm. J.	Aug. 8, 1905	36	Minear, Robert	Jun 14 1921
2	Nix, Joe C.	Aug. 8, 1905	37	Wilkens, B. Leon	Jul 1, 1921
3	Pitt, Chas. M.	Sep. 13, 1907	38	Brown, Gilbert B.	Jul 1, 1921
4	Wylie, Geo. W.	Sep 14, 1907	39	Manley, James D.	Jul 1, 1921
5	Davison, Roy	Aug. 4, 1909	40	Blackburn, John B.	Jul 5, 1921
C6	Keiser, Walter C.	Aug. 4, 1909	40	Brundage, Frank	Jul. 13, 1942
7	Slater, Elmer	Aug. 7, 1909	42	Burkarth, Geo. L.	Jul. 13, 1942
8	Duncan, Lloyd P.	Oct. 10, 1910	43	Avery, John R.	Aug. 6, 1942
9	Kiesow, Charles	Jul. 15, 1914	44	Vanselous, Russe	May 7, 1944
10	Pitch, Edw. J.	Jul. 19, 1914	45	Moore, S. R.	Jun 22, 1944
11	Parimeter, Grover	Jul. 20, 1914	46	Morhain, Mike	Apr. 10, 1945
12	Selan, Swan	Jul. 20, 1914	E47	Squyares, J. W.	Apr. 10, 1945
13	Freeman, Edgar G.	Jul. 22, 1914	48	Reed, R. L.	Apr. 23, 1945
14	Eckley, Boyd	Jul. 24, 1914	J49	Powers, R. S.	Jun 11, 1945
15	Patton, Ralph F.	Jul. 26, 1914	50	Wollard, F. M.	Jun 11, 1945
16	Maehr, G. C.	Aug. 12, 1915	51	Seal, Frank	Jul. 11, 1945
17	Meek, Wilbur J.	Aug. 26, 1915	52	Deming, Ralph	Jun 13, 1945
18	Rogers, Roy C.	Aug. 27, 1915	53	Wells, M. R.	Jun 22, 1945
19	Gerdin, Geo. P.	May 8, 1917	54	Newman, Frank L.	Jul. 8, 1945
20	Blackwell, Geo. V.	Jun 25, 1917	55	Wagner, J. J.	Jul. 8, 1945
21	Mahan, Dee F.	Aug. 13, 1917	56	Ward, E. K.	Jul. 13, 1945
22	Griswold, J. Levi	Oct. 10, 1917	57	Shere, F. E.	Jul. 20, 1945
D23	Hall, Chester	Mar. 16, 1918	58	Roberts, W. A.	Jul. 30, 1946
24	Krapf, Ernest J.	Mar. 16, 1918	59	Dempsey, W. J.	Aug. 14, 1946
25	Horton, Lou W.	Mar. 20, 1918	60	Lowery, R. H.	Aug. 14, 1946
E26	Morris, Dan	Jun 5, 1918	61	Henderson, R. W.	Aug. 19, 1946
27	Tilbury, Chas. L.	Aug. 2, 1919	62	Hall, I. C.	Aug. 19, 1946
28	Winslow, Edwin L.	Aug. 8, 1919	63	Hanson, J.	Aug. 19, 1946
29	Cekley, Byrle	Aug. 9, 1919	64	Hayes, D. L.	Aug. 20, 1946
30	Branum, L. O.	Aug. 10, 1919	65	Conrad, J. R.	Aug. 24, 1946
31	Gage, Geo. C.	Aug. 10, 1919	66	Lancaster, D. D.	Aug. 17, 1947
32	Maran, Chas. E.	Aug. 15, 1919	67	Lewis, K. R.	Aug. 17, 1947
33	Mercer, Wm E.	Sep. 4, 1920	68	Sherred, P. R.	Aug. 18, 1947
34	Morrison, Wm N.	Oct. 31, 1920	69	Arnold, E. W.	Jun. 17, 1948
35	Grimes, Otis N.	Oct. 31, 1920	H70	Ziegler, W. C.	Jun. 21, 1948

Dated July 1, 1948   Arkansas City, Kansas

(C) General Officer, Locomotive Firemen and Enginemen.

(H) Cut off road board, reduction, and returned to road firemen.

(D) Road Foreman of Engines, Middle Division

(E) Disability annuity

(G) Cut off switch board, reduction and returned to switch fireman.

THE OKLAHOAM STATE CAPITOL   JULY 25, 1907

FORTY FAMILIES OF RAILROAD MEN COMING. CHANGES IN OPERATION OF DENVER, ENID AND GULF NECESSITATES ENLARGEMENT OF YARDS.

More than forty families will be brought to Guthrie by the absorption of the Denver, Enid and Gulf railway by the Santa Fe, which took place the first of this month. The road has been operated out of Enid in the past, but the machine shops are being moved to this city and added to the south yards, and the trains will be operated out of Guthrie in the future. Already the train crews are working from here and as soon as possible they will move their families to this city.

Already there are over a hundred railroad men working out of the capitol city, and the addition of the crews of the Denver branch will bring this up to 150. In addition to the Santa Fe the Katy; Frisco ; and Fort Smith and Western; and Rock Island lay over here, composing 25 crews with 5 men to the crew. In addition to this number there are about 50 men employed in and about the local yards.

In a short time the Denver, Enid and Gulf line will be made the southern route to the Pacific Slope. Here-to-fore all this traffic has been going round by way of Arkansas City over the Eastern Oklahoma and Shawnee branches. By owning this the Santa Fe will be compelled to make extreme improvements here in the next year-in the way of enlarging the yard trackage and terminal facilities. To handle all this traffic new freight yard trackage and terminal facilities will have to be created across the Cottonwood river, on the old D.E.&G. right-of way, and the tracks on this side of the river in front of the Union Depot will be used for passenger tracks only, and train sheds will be erected at the Union Depot.

Guthrie has now over fifty scheduled passenger and local freight trains in and out of the Union Depot every 24 hours, which is more than on the main line of the Santa Fe from Kansas City to Fort Worth.

Recap of new article found in the Territorial Museum. Note spelling of Oklahoma!

Hop on the Train, young man, and stake your

Guthrie First Train Story.

Altogether ten trains got in before 3 P.M., and making allowance for those who went on to Okla.City, there must have been at least 6,000 people in Guthrie three hours after the ~~XXXXX~~ territory was legally opened to settlement.

It was wonderful the manner in which disputes were settled among the newcomers in this early part of the proceedings.

Sometimes a half dozen men would pounce on a lot. After a brief discussion, one man would be left in possession of the lot and the rest would depart to claim another lot.

BANG !!!!, the race was on for a homestead. People were hanging on all over the train. Mr Cooper pulled the throttle wide open and passed everything in sight. He made the run to Guthrie, thirty miles in thirty minutes.

Arriving in Guthrie they found people already there, but of course they were sooners.

Many jumped off the train, staked lots and stayed in Guthrie, but Mr Cooper and all the Emporia Boomers stayed on the train until it came to Seward,Oklahoma, and at that place he turned the throttle over to the regular engineer, and staked the claim where Seward,Oklahoma now stands.

Guthrie on the night of april 22nd,1889 had a population of about 15,000 to 20,000 persons.

Mr Cooper lived on the place he homesteaded until he moved to California and lived there until his death.

Before his death he gave to his son the dollar watch with which he timed the first train into Oklahoma. Later it was given to the Oklahoma State Historical Society, but someone stole it.. *****

WEDNESDAY, DEC. 9, 1998

Group to promote local preservation

By Doug McGee
The Guthrie News Leader

A committee has been formed to help save the former Rock Island Depot or the Eaton Building.

Save Our Depot, according to a news release, was formed to save historic architecture, including the Guthrie Rock Island Depot.

Guthrie businessman, Clair Stevenson, spokesman for the group said the general purpose of the group was to promote historical preservation of buildings in Guthrie.

"The specific purpose is to promote awareness of the Rock Island Depot," he said. "Part of the uniqueness of Guthrie is its old buildings. And there's only a limited number of them."

The group has established a hot-line at 282-4305, which should be operational by the weekend. Guthrie residents can call the number to get more information on the building, add their names to a newsletter mailing list or find out how they can help, Stevenson said.

"It's to give people who want to get involved access to others who are," he said. "The recording will also tell people more about the group."

Stevenson said if the caller wants they can leave comments about how they feel about the proposed demolition of the building and the group would track public opinion.

The building has gained a temporary reprieve after Guthrie resident James "Speedy" Weems filed for a restraining order against the city Monday.

Weems' attorney, John Gile, of Oklahoma City, said they obtained the order to prevent the city from issuing the demolition permit.

The restraining order was delivered to city officials Monday, City Manager Bret Jones said.

While granting the restraining order, Judge Donald Worthington set a Jan. 5 hearing date, at which time both sides will have an opportunity to be heard.

City Attorney Brian Pierson said defendants in these hearings have a chance to "show cause" why a restraining order should not continue.

"(The plaintiffs) will put on a case to make the restraining order into a temporary injunction," Pierson said.

Guthrie Depot, 1889.

ART BAUMAN

PHILIP MOSELEY PHOTO

Cimarron River bridge washout north of Guthrie, date unknown.

Guthrie, July 4, 2006.

Woman's tie to history revisited

By Ryan Piersol
The Guthrie News Leader

Ryan Piersol / The Guthrie News Leader

Margaret Leonhardt poses beside the Atchison, Topeka and Santa Fe Train Depot in downtown Guthrie. She was born upstairs in the Harvey House, where her father was a manager and her mother a waitress.

Margaret Leonhardt

Born: Nov. 14, 1905 in Guthrie
Family: Husband, Chester; two sons, Chester Jr. and Henry; six granddaughters and 14 great-grandchildren

The recent renovation of the Atchison, Topeka and Santa Fe Train Depot in downtown Guthrie is just one of many efforts taken to keep tourists attracted to the historical parts of the town.

An Edmond resident has strong ties to Guthrie's history with the train depot at Oklahoma and Fourth streets.

Margaret Leonhardt's link to Guthrie came at a time when saloons were commonly a favorite hangout, trains were a well-used form of transportation and gunfighter's were known as celebrities.

She was born on Nov. 14, 1905 in an upstairs apartment at the train depot where her family was living at the time. Her father, Kleon Egan, was manager of the Fred Harvey Restaurant, which was located beside the Sante Fe Railway.

The Fred Harvey restaurant came to Guthrie in 1903 and later became a large chain of restaurants that spread across the country. Although no Fred Harvey restaurants are currently known to be in existence, the chain lasted well into the 1960s.

Leonhardt wasn't given much time to stick around, because just four years after she was born, her father was transferred to a Fred Harvey restaurant in Jerome, Idaho. She left at such an early age that she has trouble recalling the years she spent in Guthrie, but she can always relate the stories her father used to tell her about the way Guthrie was back then.

"My father used to tell me that the trains had to stop and let the buffalo migrate by and that it could be a couple of hours. There were so many of them back then that they had to stop the train," Leonhardt said.

"He told me one time when he cooked that he prepared a quail dinner for the officials of the railroad. He was a good hunter, so he went out and got the quail and prepared it for them."

Leonhardt never got the chance to move back to Guthrie, because a few years after leaving for Idaho she moved to Oklahoma City where she has lived since. But in 1926 Guthrie became an important location in Leonhardt's life for a second time when she married Chester Leonhardt at the old court house.

The current renovations on the train depot are still on schedule with the roof construction nearly completed. According to James Martin, contractor for the Logan County Historical Society, the construction is about 20 percent finished.

Now the Leonhardt family feels like the Fred Harvey restaurant and the train depot in Guthrie are a part of the family, because it began what is now a family of more than 20 people.

"The Fred Harvey restaurant in Guthrie is where my mother and father met. She (her mother) worked for the Fred Harvey restaurant as what they called a Harvey Girl and he (Leonhardt's father) met her there while he was the manager," Leonhardt said.

The depot has been vacant for 18 years, but with the recent plans for renovation came a newfound interest in the building for the Leonhardt family. A recent visit to Guthrie provided the family an opportunity to venture into the past and see a still existing piece of family history.

The Fred Harvey 'difference'

GUTHRIE DAILY LEADER FOOTNOTE TO HISTORY MAY 1982
GUTHRIE"S OLD HARVEY HOUSE CALLED "BEST EATING AROUND" by John Wilson

FREDERICK HARVEY was fifteen years old when he left England in 1850, to try his luck in the United States. Twenty-six years later he had sampled a wandering life that had seen him working on several railroads, running his own restaurant at the Topeka station of the Santa Fe railroad. Soon Harvey had acquired 15 railroad hotels, 30 dining cars and all 47 eating places on the Santa Fe line, one of which was here in Guthrie. It was the first time an american railroad became famous for its food.

Harvey demanded style and decorum and was a perfectionest about the food and appearance of the appointments in his various establishments. If he found a chipped cup he was known to throw the table setting on the floor. Rowdy individuals were briskly ushered to the door, often by Harvey himself.

Customers not dressed for dinner were admitted only after donning neat alpaca coats which the host kept on hand for the coatless. One quotation has survived, from a Texas cowboy about the Harvey House. "They make you take off your hat and wear a coat, but the grub is strictly A-1!"

Only one incident marred the history of perfect food and service, and Guthrie has the questionable honor of being the scene of that incident.. Imagine the train station early in the morning stillness of summer 1893, with lanterns still glowing in the windows of the side-tracked work cars as the gandy dancers try to wake up. On a siding, an engine being fired up and a few passengers standing around on the platform.
The early train pulls in and the half light tired passengers walk in silence to the Harvey House anticipating the famous food and fresh hot coffee. Sitting at tables, yearning to "clean up", they watch as the "Waiter Girls" as they were called

came from the kitchen and began to pour the hot coffee into the immaculate white cups with the Harvey House Shield tastefully emblazoned on the side.

Now imagine what people felt, thought, and spontaneously said when baby frogs began jumping out of the cups of steaming coffee onto clothes, into pockets, hats and handbags, and finally onto the floor,--dozens that at that time seemed like hundreds.!!

Frederick Henry Harvey hired the famous Pinkerton Agency to find the culprit who had obviously sneaked into the kitchen very, very early that morning and placed the frogs in the cups. Alas, the culprit, real or convenient was never found. There was, however a brakeman who had worked in the Guthrie yards for several years and who was known to have a sense of humor known now as "offbeat" and then as simply unconventional--who continued to work for the line another fifteen years, but never again entered the Harvey House.

The north end of the Guthrie station where the Harvey House once flourished is now prosaically used by the "Work Section" of the Santa Fe, and the lights no longer glisten over snowy linens, and the aroma of coffee comes only in the imagination of those who love history.

Since passenger service was discontinued two years ago with the removal of Amtrak "LONE STAR", the question has been bruited about among railroad and history fans,"could the station perhaps be leased from the railroad for some more interesting use?.

To those gifted with imagination however, the sound of the trains clicking by in a furious attempt to "catch their whistles" needs only the lighting of lamps to conjure up the visions of crisply aproned "waiter girls" gliding between the elegant tables dispensing elegant food. The last gleams of the sun mingle with the street lights to trace a golden pattern on the windows of the station, a dim mirror of the well used polished silver, sparkling crystal and freshly laundered linens that once lent the ambience that made Guthrie's Harvey house the finest eating place in the area.

PHILIP MOSELEY PHOTO

A fine example of a railroad house in Guthrie, July 4, 2006.

OKLAHOMA RAILWAY MUSEUM

Santa Fe yard in Guthrie, OK, circa 1906, looking north from coaling facility. Engine in foreground appears to be #2373, a 2-8-0 built by Taunton in 1882 as Santa Fe #273. Engine was scrapped in 1914. Photo provided by Nita Wainscott, courtesy of The Oklahoma Territorial Museum.

Riding the rails …a perilous choice, then and now.

THE GUTHRIE DAILY LEADER

MARCH 26, 1896
JUMPED ON CARS AND RECEIVED INJURIES WHICH MAY PROVE FATAL.

ACCIDENT TO A BOY.

Will Mock the 16 year old son of M.L.Mock, was badly hurt and narrowly escaped being ground to pieces by a Santa Fe train yesterday. Mock, with a number of other boys who play about the railroad yards daily and court death, attempted to board a freight to ride to the new Cimarron bridge. The other boys mounted safely, but y9ung Mock slipped and fell and was struck a terrific jolt in the head by the cars. He was rendered unconsious and only the quick work of bystanders saved him from a horrible death.

The lad received two ugly wounds in the head and may not survive the accidant.

Form 2532 Standard - Boiler Form No. 1   75M—12-25—C

Santa Fe
Atchison Topeka & Santa Fe Ry Co
(Insert name of Railway Company)

MONTHLY LOCOMOTIVE INSPECTION AND REPAIR REPORT

Month of **July**, 192 **6**   Locomotive { Number **3123** / Initial **AT & SF** }

Atchison Topeka & Santa Fe Ry Company

In accordance with the act of Congress approved February 17, 1911, as amended March 4, 1915, and the rules and instructions issued in pursuance thereof and approved by the Interstate Commerce Commission, all parts of locomotive No. **3123**, including the boiler and appurtenances, were inspected on **July 29th**, 192 **6**, at **Guthrie, Oklahoma**, and all defects disclosed by said inspection have been repaired, except as noted on the back of this report.

1. Steam gauges tested and left in good condition on **July 29**, 192 **6**
2. Safety valves set to pop at **200** pounds, **202** pounds, **205** pounds on **July 29**, 192 **6**
3. Were both injectors tested and left in good condition? **Yes**
4. Were steam leaks repaired? **Yes**
5. Condition of brake and signal equipment **Good Not Used**
6. Condition of draft gear and draw gear **Good Good, R&I. 7-29-26**
7. Condition of driving gear **Good**
8. Condition of running gear **Good**
9. Condition of tender **Good**
10. Was boiler washed and gauge cocks and water glass cock spindles removed and cocks cleaned? **Yes Yes Yes**
11. Were steam leaks repaired? **Yes**
12. Condition of staybolts and crown stays **Good Good**
13. Number of staybolts and crown stays renewed **None None**
14. Condition of flues and fire-box sheets **Good Good**
15. Condition of arch and water bar tubes, if used **Good Not Used**
16. Were fusible plugs removed and cleaned? **Not Used**
17. Date of previous hydrostatic test **May 21st**, 192 **6**
18. Date of removal of caps from flexible staybolts **May 27**, 192 **6**

I certify that the above report is correct. Items **1 to 10. Incl.** _____ Inspector

I certify that the above report is correct. Items **9 to 18. Incl.** _____ Inspector

State of **Oklahoma**
County of **Logan** } ss:

Subscribed and sworn to before me this **31st** day of **July**, 192 **6**, by { **W L Willoby** / **C E Hollar** } inspectors of the **Atchison Topeka & Santa Fe Ry** Company.

My Commission Expires, **October 7th, 1928**.

Clyde B Weaver, Notary Public.

The above work has been performed and the report is approved.

_____ Officer in Charge.

Form 2532 Standard—Boiler Form No. 1 75M—12-25—C

Santa Fe
Atchison Topeka & Santa Fe Ry Co
(Insert name of Railway Company)

MONTHLY LOCOMOTIVE INSPECTION AND REPAIR REPORT

Month of **July**, 192 **6** Locomotive { Number **3115** / Initial **AT & SF** }

Atchison Topeka & Santa Fe Ry Company

In accordance with the act of Congress approved February 17, 1911, as amended March 4, 1915, and the rules and instructions issued in pursuance thereof and approved by the Interstate Commerce Commission, all parts of locomotive No. **3115**, including the boiler and appurtenances, were inspected on **July 25th**, 192 **6**, at **Guthrie, Oklahoma**, and all defects disclosed by said inspection have been repaired, except as noted on the back of this report.

1. Steam gauges tested and left in good condition on **July 25**, 192 **6**
2. Safety valves set to pop at **200** pounds, **202** pounds, **205** pounds on **July 25**, 192 **6**
3. Were both injectors tested and left in good condition? **Yes**
4. Were steam leaks repaired? **Yes**
5. Condition of brake and signal equipment **Good Not Used**
6. Condition of draft gear and draw gear **Good Good, R&I. 7-25-26**
7. Condition of driving gear **Good**
8. Condition of running gear **Good**
9. Condition of tender **Good**

10. Was boiler washed and gauge cocks and water glass cock spindles removed and cocks cleaned? **Yes Yes Yes**
11. Were steam leaks repaired? **Yes**
12. Condition of staybolts and crown stays **Good Good**
13. Number of staybolts and crown stays renewed **None None**
14. Condition of flues and fire-box sheets **Good Good**
15. Condition of arch and water bar tubes, if used **Good Not Used**
16. Were fusible plugs removed and cleaned? **Not Used**
17. Date of previous hydrostatic test **May 16th**, 192 **5**
18. Date of removal of caps from flexible staybolts **May 13**, 192 **4**

I certify that the above report is correct.
Items 1 to 10 Incl. _____, Inspector

I certify that the above report is correct.
Items #9 to 18 Incl. _____, Inspector

State of **Oklahoma**
County of **Logan** } ss:

Subscribed and sworn to before me this **27th** day of **July**, 192 **6**, by { **D D Gray** / **C E Hollar** }, inspectors of the **Atchison Topeka & Santa Fe Ry** Company.

My Commission Expires, **October 7th, 1928**.

Clyde B Weaver, Notary Public.

The above work has been performed and the report is approved.

_____, Officer in Charge.

(Over)

The First 'Great Land Rush' Train in Oklahoma...

THE FIRST TRAIN by EVELYNN L. SORTAIN

Thirty miles in thirty minutes was a record breaking speed in the days of yesterday, and at this speed George Cooper drove the first train into Oklahoma. Mr Cooper was a captain of Payne's Oklahoma Colony Camp No. 2 of Emporia, Kansas, and through his popularity he received a special permit from the Santa Fe officials to take care of the throttle and run the first train into Oklahoma from the north on April 22, 1889.

The train arrived in the Cherokee Strip about two miles north of where the town of Orlando now stands.

It was nearing the zero hour of 12 o-clock and the people were milling about like ants, waiting for the signal which would send them dashing for new homes. Women were pushing; babies were screaming; men were ready for take-off. Many of the people were horse-back, some were in buggies, Oklahoma Boomer wagons, and afoot.

Many on foot tried to crowd into Mr Cooper's train. The train was so crowded no one could get inside, so they climbed on top of the train, on the cow-catcher, (or pilot), tender and in the cab of the engine. Mr Cooper had an exasperating time clearing the cab so he could drive the steam horse at it's fastest gait. The people were so impatient that they could hardly wait for the train to pull out for the new land.

…was a record-breaker, speeding along at 'thirty miles in thirty minutes'.

Finally 12 o-clock came by railroad time, which was taken from St.Louis,Missouri time, and about twenty-five minutes faster than Sun,or Meridian time, ~~but he obeyed~~ The crowd got so exicited and restless that they yelled at the soldiers, "Shoot and let's go!!",but the soldiers would not let them pass until 12 o-clock noon,sun time, then they snarled at Mr Cooper for not going by railroad time, but he obeyed orders of Uncle Sam's soldiers and waited for the legal time in order not to be sooners.

Altogether ten trains got in before 3 P.M., and making allowance for those who went on to Okla.City, there must have been at least 6,000 people in Guthrie three hours after the territory was legally opened to settlement.

It was wonderful the manner in which disputes were settled among the newcomers in this early part of the proceedings.

Sometimes a half dozen men would pounce on a lot. After a brief discussion, one man would be left in possession of the lot and the rest would depart to claim another lot.

Wells Fargo Office at Guthrie, Oklahoma c. 1889.

GUTHRIE TERRITORIAL MUSEUM

SANTA FE RAILWAY ARCHIVES

Guthrie Santa Fe Freight depot, 1940.

COURTESY PHIL MORROW COLLECTION

B-9-66-350M **Santa Fe** Form 1016 Standard

TRACK CAR OPERATOR'S LINE-UP OF TRAINS

STATION __GUTHRIE__

LINE-UP OF TRAINS expected between stations __GUTHRIE__ and __ENID__
between the hours of __645A__ M and __5P__ M, Date __JUNE 16__, 19__72__

Westward or Southward Trains:

EX 274C WORK TRAIN WITH RAIL LEAVE KIOWA 9 AM CHEROKEE 930A BLANTON 11A

THEN WORKS BETWEEN ENID AND DOUGLAS

EX 275 WEST 1453 KIOWA 10AM CHEROKEE 1045A BLANTON 100P

EX 278 NO 1455 KIOWA 1100AM CHEROKEE 1130A BLANTON 200P

EX 25

Eastward or Northward Trains:

EX 253 C EAST 2510 LEFT GUTHRIE 625A ENID 900AM

EX 275 NO 1454 BLANTON 700AM CHEROKEE 830A KIOWA 900AM

EX 221 BLANTON 715A CHEROKEE 830A KIOWA 900AM

EX 214 NO 1456 BLANTON 830A CHEROKEE 10 AM KIOWA 1030A

WK EX 274C BETWEEN DOUGLAS AND ENID AFTER 11 AM

SPS WB 650A

RECORD OF MAIN TRACK OCCUPANCY

LOCATION	TIME TRACK CAR PLACED ON TRACK	TIME CAR IN CLEAR	LOCATION
	M	M	
	M	M	
	M	M	
	M	M	
	M	M	

This line-up has been read aloud to all other occupants of track car.

_____
Track Car Operator

Note: A separate sheet should be used for each line-up secured during each work period.

Guthrie station track chart from Russell Crump.

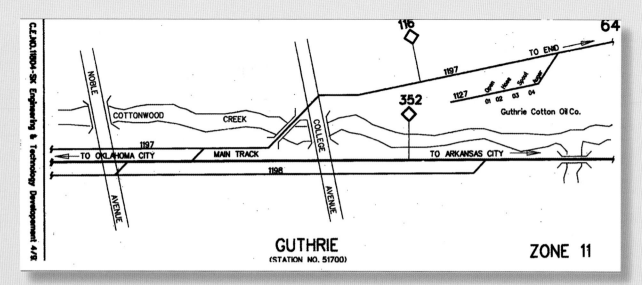

Guthrie, c. 1965, Carl Graves photo.

TERRITORIAL MUSEUM ARCHIVES

A sod mansion in Guthrie, Oklahoma.

AUTHOR PHOTO

Eastern Oklahoma Railway end of track, 1966, near Camp Russell, Oklahoma.

A. T. & S. F. Ry.

TRACK CONNECTIONS AND JOINT POINTS WITH OTHER LINES—(CONT'D).

NOTE.—Heavy Black Type Indicates No Track Connections Whatever.

STATIONS	Names of Connecting or Joint Lines
GOWER..............Mo.	St. Joseph & Grand Island Ry.
GREAT BEND.....Kan.	**Missouri Pacific Ry.**
GREENLAND......Colo.	**Denver & Rio Grande R. R.**
GRIDLEY...........Kan.	**Missouri Pacific Ry.**
GUTHRIE..........Okla.	M. K. & T. Ry.—St. L. E. R. & W. Ry.
" "	Ft. Smith & Western R. R.—C. R. I. & P. Ry.
HARDIN.............Mo.	Wabash R. R.
HARPER............Kan.	K. C. M. & O. Ry.
HAZELTON........ "	**Missouri Pacific Ry.**
HOPE................ "	**Chicago, Burlington & Quincy R. R.**
HUMBOLDT....... "	**Missouri, Kansas & Texas Ry.**
HURDLAND........Mo.	Q. O. & K. C. R. R.
HUSTED.............Colo.	**Denver & Rio Grande R. R.**
HUTCHINSON...Kan.	C. R. I. & P. Ry.—Mo. Pac. Ry.
INDEPENDENCE... "	Missouri Pacific Ry.
IOLA.................. "	Missouri Pacific Ry.
" "	M. K. & T. Ry.
ILETA...............N. M.	A. T. & S. F. Ry. (Coast Lines).
JACOBS.............Kan.	Chicago, Rock Island & Pacific Ry.
JANSEN.............Colo.	Colo. & Wy. Ry.—D. & R. G. R. R. via A. T. & S. F. main line, Trinidad to C. & W. yard.
JOLIET..............Ill.	Mich. Cent. R. R.—C. & A. Ry.—E. J. & E. Ry.
" "	C. L. S. & E. Ry.—Chicago, Rock Island & Pacific Ry.
KANSAS CITY....Mo.	K. C. Belt Ry.—Frisco System—C. B. & Q. R. R.
" "	C. M. & St. P. Ry.—C. & A. Ry.—C. R. I. & P. Ry.
" "	Mo. Pacific Ry.—Wabash R. R.—U. P. R. R.
" "	M. K. & T. Ry. via Frisco System.
" "	K. C. S. Ry. via Sheffield.
" "	Q. O. & K. C. Ry. via Sheffield and K. C. S. Ry.
" "	St. J. & G. I. Ry. via Sheffield and K. C. S. Ry.
" "	C. G. W. R. R. via Frisco System, Mo. Pac. Ry. or K. C. S. Ry.
KELLOGG..........Kan.	**Missouri Pacific Ry.**
KENNEDY..........N. M	New Mexico Central Ry.
KINGMAN..........Kan	**Missouri Pacific Ry.**
KIOWA.............. "	**Missouri Pacific Ry.**
LANSING........... "	Mo. Pac. Ry.—Union Pacific R. R.
LA PLATA..........Mo.	Wabash R. R.
LARKSPUR.........Colo.	**Denver & Rio Grande R. R.**
LARNED............Kan.	**Missouri Pacific Ry.**
LA ROSE............Ill.	**Chicago & Alton Ry.**
LATHROP...........Mo.	Chicago, Burlington & Quincy R. R.
LAWRENCE........Kan.	**Union Pacific R. R.**
LAWSON...........Mo.	Chicago, Milwaukee & St. Paul Ry.
LEAVENWORTH..Kan.	Leavenworth & Topeka Ry.
" "	C. B. & Q. R. R.—C. R. I. & P. Ry. } via L. & T. Ry.
" "	U. P. R. R.—Mo. Pac. Ry.
LEMONT............Ill.	**Chicago & Alton Ry.**
LEXINGTON JCT..Mo.	Wabash R. R.
LINDSAY...........Okla.	C. R. I. & P. Ry.
LITTLETON........Colo.	**Denver & Rio Grande R. R.**
LOCKPORT.........Ill.	**Chicago & Alton Ry.**
LOMAX............. "	**Chicago, Burlington & Quincy R. R.**
LORENZO.......... "	**Chicago and Alton Ry.**
LORRAINE........Kan.	**Frisco System.**
LOST SPRINGS... "	**Chicago, Rock Island & Pacific Ry.**
LYNDON............ "	**Missouri Pacific Ry.**

A. T. & S. F. Ry.

TRACK CONNECTIONS AND JOINT POINTS WITH OTHER LINES—(CONT'D).

NOTE.—Heavy Black Type Indicates No Track Connections Whatever.

STATIONS	Names of Connecting or Joint Lines
LYONS...............Kan.	Frisco System.—Missouri Pacific Ry.
MADISON........... "	**Missouri Pacific Ry.**
MARION............. "	**Chicago, Rock Island & Pacific Ry.**
MAZON..............Ill.	Cleveland, Cincinnati, Chicago & St. Louis Ry.
McCOOK............. "	C. T. T. R. R.
" "	Indiana Harbor Belt R. R. } via C. T. T. R. R.
" "	Chicago & Ills. Western Ry.
McPHERSON......Kan.	C. R. I. & P. Ry.—U. P. R. R.
" "	Mo. Pac. Ry. via U. P. R. R.
MEDFORD..........Okla.	Chicago, Rock Island & Pacific Ry.
MEDILL.............Mo.	Chicago, Burlington & Quincy R. R.
MERIDEN..........Kan.	Leavenworth & Topeka Ry.
MILITARY POST..Colo.	**Denver & Rio Grande R. R.**
MILLSDALE........ "	Chicago & Alton Ry.
MILTONVALE.....Kan.	**Leavenworth, Kansas & Western Ry.**
MINNEAPOLIS.... "	Union Pacific R. R.
MINONK............Ill.	Illinois Central R. R.
MONICA............. "	**Chicago, Burlington & Quincy R. R.**
MONUMENT......Colo.	**Denver & Rio Grande R. R.**
MORTON...........Ill.	Terre Haute & Indianapolis R. R.
NEMO................ "	Iowa Central Ry.
NEOSHO FALLS...Kan.	**Missouri, Kansas & Texas Ry.**
NEPESTA...........Colo.	Missouri Pacific Ry.
NERSKA............Ill.	Belt Ry. of Chicago.
NEW CAMBRIA...Kan.	C. R. I. & P. Ry.—**Union Pacific R. R.**
NEWTON........... "	Missouri Pacific Ry.
NICKERSON...... "	Missouri Pacific Ry.
NIMROD.............Mo.	Wabash R. R.
NIOTAZE...........Kan.	Missouri Pacific Ry
NORBORNE........Mo.	Wabash R. R.
NORTH TOPEKA.Kan.	C. R. I. & P. Ry.—Union Pacific R. R.
NORWICH.......... "	**Missouri Pacific Ry.**
OKLAHOMA CITY..Okla.	C. R. I. & P. Ry.—M. K. & T. Ry.—Frisco System.
OLATHE............Kan.	Frisco System—K. C. C. & S. Ry.
OSAGE CITY...... "	Missouri Pacific Ry.
OTTAWA........... "	Missouri Pacific Ry.
OXFORD............ "	**Missouri Pacific Ry.**
PALEMON..........Mo.	Wabash R. R.
PALMER LAKE...Colo.	Denver & Rio Grande R. R.
PARNELL..........Kan.	**Missouri Pacific Ry.**
PARTRIDGE....... "	**Chicago, Rock Island & Pacific Ry.**
PAULS VALLEY...Okla.	G. C. & S. F. Ry.
PAWNEE............ "	Frisco System.
PEABODY..........Kan.	**Chicago, Rock Island & Pacific Ry.**
PECK................. "	**Chicago, Rock Island & Pacific Ry.**
PEKIN...............Ill.	C. C. C. & St. L. Ry.—C. & A. Ry.
" "	P. R. T. Co.—P. & P. U. Ry. } via C. C. C. & St. L. Ry.
" "	C. P. & St. L. Ry.
PEQUOT............. "	Chicago & Alton Ry.
PERRY..............Okla.	Frisco System.
PERTH..............Kan.	**Chicago, Rock Island & Pacific Ry.**
PERU................ "	**Missouri Pacific Ry.**
PINON...............Colo.	D. & R. G. R. R.
PITTSBURG.......Kan.	Mo. Pac. Ry. Frisco System.—K. C. S. Ry.
PLAINES............Ill.	C. & A. Ry.
PLATTSBURG......Mo.	C. R. I. & P. Ry.—Q. O. & K. C. R. R.
POMONA...........Kan.	**Missouri Pacific Ry.**
PORTLAND.......Colo.	Denver & Rio Grande R. R.
PRATT..............Kan.	**Chicago, Rock Island & Pacific Ry.**

Copy of Santa Fe passenger train connections sheet. Note Guthrie above left.

Maurice Rouse published two works covering the history of Cowboy Flat, an area south of the Cimarron River, east of Guthrie and west of Coyle, Oklahoma. His parents were Eighty-Niners who lived in Pleasant Valley. He was born on their homestead in 1893, and lived there all his life. He wrote about the Doolin Gang and how Bittercreek Newcomb, a gang member, sold his homestead stake to the Rouses. Maurice operated a cotton gin in Pleasant Valley. It is now a ghost town. Rouse remembered when the Eastern Oklahoma Railway laid its tracks through town, establishing a small depot and a siding. He also witnessed its dismantling. Maurice was a close friend of the outlaw Bill Doolin's son, who became a minister. Thanks to their efforts, Bill Doolin's grave at the Guthrie cemetery is now marked by a fine tombstone, replacing an old wagon axle stuck previously at that site.

Doolin was a popular figure in the Guthrie area, despite being a bandit chief. Probably, some people felt a bit of civic pride in the fact that he headed the last of the big western outlaw gangs. Shortly before his demise, Doolin had been captured by **Bill Tilghman**. Tighlman, **Chris Madsen and Heck Thomas**, known as "The Guardsmen", were a famous trio of western lawmen selected by **Evitt D. Nix**, the first U.S. Marshall appointed at Guthrie. Their assigned task was to clean up the renegades and outlaws who rampaged through I.T. and O.T. They succeeded. Many of these brigands were shot by lawmen or hanged by **Judge Isaac Parker**, holding court in Fort Smith, Arkansas.

Lawman Tighlman transported his prisoner to Guthrie via the Santa Fe. They were met by a cheering and admiring crowd at the depot. These celebrating worthies, including some swooning women, directed their enthusiasm toward Doolin, not Tighlman! A short time later, Doolin escaped jail and fled eastward to the Quay area over the future grade of the Eastern Oklahoma Railway. Unbeknownst to poor Bill, he had sealed his doom, as the lawmen decided to take no further chances with him if captured again. In 1893, a posse caught him in Quay and shot him to death in front of his wife and young son.

Pleasant Valley/Cowboy Flat historian and my friend, Maurice C. Rouse at the Fogarty home in 1967.

AUTHOR PHOTO

Our Times
Viewed by WAYNE MACKEY
Oklahoma City Times, May 6, 1970.

TWO OLD TIMERS took a sentimental journey the other day. C. M. Thompson of El Reno, who'll be 80 rather soon, and Leon Townsend, 66, of Oklahoma City, retraced part of an old railroad line that most people don't even realize ever existed.

Mr. Thompson is an old-time Rock Island conductor, and Mr. Townsend is an old-time postal worker. Both are retired now, of course.

They are more or less experts on the old St. Louis, El Reno & Western railroad which until it was abandoned in 1922 operated haphazardly between Guthrie and El Reno. Neither ever rode the line, but Mr. Thompson operated alongside it for quite a while and Mr. Townsend used to sack mail for towns along the railway.

Wayne Mackey

Some of the towns, of course, have now disappeared.

Along for the ride as the two backtracked the old roadbed was Eldon Smith, 70, an Oklahoma City friend of Mr. Townsend. We tagged along, too.

☆ ☆ ☆ ☆

THE OLD St. Louis, El Reno & Western was built in 1903. It was one of those operations that occurred pretty frequently in those days.

Some fellow hit it lucky, promoted funds to build a short railway and then hoped to sell it to a larger company to be integrated into a long line.

Well, the St. Louis, El Reno & Western cost $817,000 to build, but no buyer was available.

There were 42 miles of track, one steam engine, two passenger cars, one express-mail car and two cabooses listed when the line shut down. Two men operated the whole thing, an engineer and a conductor. The latter also served as brakeman.

Leon Townsend

ANYWAY, a lot of cotton gins, grain elevators and the like sprung up along the line. But only in one year, 1919, did the railway show a profit, and even that was rather small.

Finally, Carl Humphries, president of the El Reno Mill & Elevator Co. was appointed in 1920 as receiver for the line.

His reaction two years later after trying to make it pay?

"I wish I had never heard of the El Reno & Western."

☆ ☆ ☆ ☆

OUR GROUP drove section line roads the other day, zig-zagging northeastward from El Reno, picking up traces of the old roadbed across pastures and so forth. It's surprising how many farmer have scooped out earth from behind the roadbed to form farm ponds.

We followed it quite a ways beyond Piedmont before deciding we'd had enough. We might go back some time and trace it the rest of the way.

Mr. Townsend, by the way, was with the postal service from 1919 to 1958. Mr. Thompson was with Rock Island from 1911 to 1956.

C. M. Thompson

Mr. Thompson recalls that back in the days the railroad was in operation, a man used to be borrowed from Rock Island once in a while — if either the engineer or conductor of the St. Louis, El Reno & Western had to have a day off.

Anyway, when the line was shut down, the rails, ties and equipment weren't salvaged until 1926 and 1927. It left a lot of elevators and the like high and dry. Even in Piedmont, one of the surviving towns, grain is hauled now by truck.

What a wonderful trip to jog memories.

Mr. **Jack Pfisterer** graciously provided another anecdote of train travel in Oklahoma to complete this chapter:

While I was in Ark City (Arkansas City, Kansas) the high school band and the local riding club regularly participated in Guthrie's 89er celebration each April and the riding club and high school band from Guthrie reciprocated for Ark City's "Arkalalah" celebration each October. The Ark City delegation traveled by means of two coaches and two "horse express" cars attached to AT&SF trains 27 and 28. The cars were usually attached to the end of the trains because they passed through Guthrie outside of the hours of the Guthrie switch crew. This minimized switching moves for the road crew.

During the tip to Guthrie, many of the band and riding club members would go forward through the Pullman cars to the combination diner-club car for breakfast. (That car also was switched into the train at Ark City after laying over from Number 28 some six hours earlier.) Until near the end of steam operations, Guthrie had a little 2-6-0 switcher with a slope back tender and a big number. (It originally was numbered in the 2000 class, but the Santa Fe wanted to use that series of numbers for diesel switchers and re-numbered the six wheel switchers to the 9000s by adding 7000 to their original numbers.) A single switching crew manned it during the daylight hours.

During 89er Days, the switch crew's first chore was to pick up the Ark City coaches dropped by Number 27 and move them to a team track south of the station. During the day, the band and the riding club operated out of the cars, using the horse express cars as stables and the coaches as headquarters, day rooms and dressing rooms. The coaches we used were divided into two or three compartments which facilitated the dressing room use. Apparently, they were set up in that manner for "Jim Crow" needs, as one compartment contained a sign that could be flipped to read either "White" or "Colored." At the end of the day, the switch crew's final chore was to move the Ark City cars back to a siding where Number 28 could couple onto them for the return to Ark City.

*I was already a railfan and railroad modeler at that time, so took special pleasure in the railroad aspects of the visits. In my last year, the huge Santa Fe 3460 class **Hudsons** (4-6-4) had been relegated to handling trains 27 and 28, so I had the pleasure of riding to (and probably from) Guthrie behind Number 3463.*

*The schedules of Trains 11 and 12 (**The Kansas Citian**) and The Chicago "streamliners" would have worked for the good citizens of Guthrie attending "Arkalalah" in October, but the Santa Fe apparently was not taken with the idea of having heavyweight coaches and horse express cars added to them. So, Guthrie got its own special trains traveling a little behind 11 and 12.*

*I usually went down to the station to see the **Guthrie Special** arrive in the morning and as I recall, it was always handled by one of the lanky **Atlantic** engines (4-4-2) stationed around the system by the Santa Fe as "protection" (emergency replacements) for disabled passenger train locomotives. Those Atlantics were rather strange in that their main rods were connected to the front drivers, making them appreciably longer than most Atlantic types; in effect, an **American Standard** (4-4-0) with an added trailer truck.*

*The preceding reminds me about the only time I saw engine Number 3460 (the sole streamlined member of the class) while it was in the Ark City roundhouse. Its electric generator had failed as it was leaving Ark City with Train 28 the previous night. Train 28 left for Kansas City behind Ark City's protection locomotive, **Pacific** 3403. The Ark City shop replaced the generator in time for Train 27 that night.*

Harold Loucks, my former Junior High School principal and longtime railfan, learned of 3460's unplanned visit. He called me and we went down to the roundhouse together. Engine 3460 was too long for the turntable, so had been run into one of the stalls that aligned with a lead track. While I examined the monster, Mr. Loucks engaged a shop employee in conversation. Shortly, to my surprise, I heard the turntable start up and then align with 3460's stall. One of the shop men then backed the engine onto the turntable so that we could take pictures! Those were the days.

continued on page 134

S. R. WOOD PHOTO

Guthrie Engine House, c. 1938.

CHRISTOPHER PALMIERI PHOTO

Christopher Palmieri shot this nifty scene of the *Heartland Flyer* at Oklahoma City in early 2007.

Jack Pfisterer, continued from page 132

For some reason, Loucks was enamored with the Santa Fe's 3500 class Pacifics that were rarely seen (if ever) in Ark City. Perhaps to compensate for their local absence, his automobile license plates always featured the number 3500, and most of the school teachers had plates with 3500 numbers, also.

Locomotives of one class of Santa Fe **Mikados** *(2-8-2 types of either 3100 or 3219 class) had a tendency to whistle while they worked; no, not the steam whistle, the exhaust—and just a few of them. I remember one of the whistlers showing up in Guthrie on the* **"Guthrie Turn"** *one 89er Day. This train was a local freight that operated roundtrip daily from Ark City to Guthrie.*

The 89er Days featured a long morning parade, with the rest of the day and evening devoted to a street carnival and various entertainments. To help while away the time awaiting train 28, the Ark City band made it a practice to suit up and parade about the carnival area briefly in the early evening. One year, some rowdies began following and heckling the band during its march. That ended very quickly when members of the Roundup Club saw what was happening and formed a couple of extra ranks on the rear of the band.

The last time I made the trip, train 28 added the Ark City cars to the end of its consist, as usual. Then, the crew produced an extra pair of marker lamps that they installed and plugged in on the rear, leaving the original markers in place and plugged in on the last Pullman car. We made the run to Ark City with two sets of marker lamps illuminated! Never saw anything like that before or since.

"Oh, what a beautiful mornin'…"

Oklahoma celebrated its centennial in January 2007 with the release of an official Oklahoma Statehood Stamp showing sunrise over the Cimarron River painted by Chickasaw artist Mike Larsen.

AUTHOR PHOTO

Cimarron River in 1966 from Horse Thief Canyon.

References

Bauman, Art: Data from Santa Fe Railway archives, Enid, OK.

Bryant, Keith L. Jr.: *History of the Atchison, Topeka and Santa Fe Railway.* University of Nebraska Press, Lincoln, NE, 1974.

Bryant, Keith L. Jr.: Railroad Redundant: The Fort Smith & Western Railway. *Railroad History, No. 174.* The Railway and Locomotives Historical Society, Westford, MA, Spring 1996.

Burchardt, Bill: Four Hundred and Fogarty, *Oklahoma Today,* Vol. XIX, No 1, Winter, 1963-1964.

Chandler, Allison and Maguire, Stephen D.: *When Oklahoma Took the Trolley.* Interurbans Publications, Glendale, CA, 1980.

Crump, Russell: Data and records from Santa Fe Railway archives, Shawnee Mission, KS.

Dorman, Richard Lee: Railroad book publishing data, Santa Fe, NM.

Draper, William R.: *The Last Government Land Lottery.* Haldeman-Julius Publications, Girard, KS, 1946.

Flynn, Streeter B., Jr.: Data from Santa Fe Railway archives, Oklahoma City, OK.

Forbes, Gerald: Guthrie: *Oklahoma's First Capital.* University of Oklahoma Press, No.3, Norman, OK, 1938.

George, Preston, and Wood, Sylvan R.: *The Railroads of Oklahoma, No. 60.* The Railway and Locomotive Historical Society, Boston, MA, 1943.

Gibbs, Lawrence: Data from *Stillwater News Press* archives, Stillwater, OK.

Guthrie Territorial Museum: Photos, articles, data. Guthrie, OK.

Harrington, Fred Harvey*: Hanging Judge.* University of Oklahoma Press, Norman, OK, 1996.

Hofsommer, Donovan L.: *Railroads in Oklahoma.* Oklahoma Historical Society, Oklahoma City, OK, 1977.

Hoig, Stan: *The Oklahoma Land Rush of 1889.* Oklahoma Historical Society, Oklahoma City, OK, 1984.

Kirk, John B. Jr.: Unpublished data from AT&SF and DE&G and FS&W archives, Oklahoma City, OK.

The Leader, Guthrie, Oklahoma, various articles.

Lentz, Lloyd C. III: *Guthrie: A History of the Capital City 1889-1910*, Logan County Historical Society, Guthrie, OK, 1990.

McGuire, Lloyd H., Jr.: *Birth of Guthrie: Oklahoma's Run of 1889 and Life in Guthrie in 1889 and the 1890,* Second Edition, San Diego, CA, 2000.

Masterson, V.V.: *The Katy Railroad and the Last Frontier.* University of Oklahoma Press, Norman, OK, 1952.

Moore, John B., Jr.: Photos and data. Albuquerque, NM.

Morris, John W.: *Ghost Towns of Oklahoma.* University of Oklahoma Press, Norman, OK, 1978.

National Railway Publication Company: *The Official Guide to Railways, 1902, 1903, 1910, 1920, 1933, 1940, 1965.* New York.

Rand McNally: *Handy Railroad Atlas of the United States* (Reprint). Carstens Publications, Newton NJ, 1974.

Read, Robert: Historical railroad data. Cushing, OK.

Rouse, Maurice D.: *A History of Cowboy Flat-Campbell, Pleasant Valley 1889-1960.* Coyle, OK, 1961.

Shearer Publishing: *The Roads of Oklahoma.* Fredricksburg, TX, 1997.

Shirk, George L.: *Oklahoma Place Names, Second Edition.* University of Oklahoma Press, Norman, OK, 1987.

Worley, E.D.: *Iron Horses of the Santa Fe Trail.* Southwest Railroad Historical Society, Dallas, TX 1965.

Index

8-wheeler   43
89er Days   132–134
10-wheeler   43

A
advertisement   75, 91
Amtrak   7, 8, 102, 103, 109
Atchison, Topeka & Santa Fe Railroad (ATSF or AT&SF)   12, 14, 20, 33, 35, 36, 42, 43, 50, 51, 55, 65, 86, 110, 120, 121, 132
Atlantic & Pacific Railroad   19
automobile, car, motor vehicle   26, 35, 61, 63, 64, 65, 97, 100

B
Baldwin Locomotive Works   43
Blackwell & Southern Railway   20
Blanton, W.D.   17
Blanton Junction   17, 47, 48, 64
boxcar   11
Brooks Opera House   97
Burlington Northern Railroad (now Burlington Northern Santa Fe, BNSF)   12, 24, 40, 54, 55, 60, 61, 64, 75

C
caboose: DE&G 45; Frisco 6; FS&W 85
Cashion, Roy   31
Cashion Local Line   32
Chandler Branch (Rock Island line)   34
Cherokee Depot   17, 63
Cherokee Strip (land)   122

Chicago, Rock Island & Pacific Railroad   12, 31. See also Peavine, Rock Island
Choctaw, Oklahoma & Gulf Railroad (former Choctaw, Oklahoma & Western)   5, 12, 31, 32, 37, 56, 71, 72
Cimarron River   13, 20, 23, 26, 46, 52, 114, 130, 134, 135
Cimarron Valley Historical Society   6
Cimarron Valley Museum (former Yale Depot)   6
claim jumper   10
Classen, A.H.   97
Clinton, Oklahoma & Western Railroad   56
club car   132
coal field   32
coal dock   42
coaling tower   36
common stock (certificates)   16, 44, 76, 81
conductor   7, 17, 25, 69
connection(s)   23, 64, 129
Cooper, George (engineer)   122–123
cotton   21, 32, 35
cow catcher   122
Coyle Cotton Gin   21
Crescent Depot   46
Cushing Christmas parade   6

D
DeGolyer, Everett   23
Denver, Enid & Gulf Railroad (DE&G)   7, 11, 17, 43, 44, 45, 48, 61, 62, 64
Dolese Sand Company   26

Doodlebug (D'Bug) 7, 46, 103
Doolin Gang 130
Doolin, William (Bill) 130
Douglas Depot 7

E

Eastern Oklahoma Railway (Railroad) 6, 10, 11, 13, 20, 22, 23, 24, 27, 29, 32, 35, 43, 60, 75, 81, 128, 130
Egan, Kleon 115
Eighty-Niners 130
Electric Park 97
El Reno Mill & Elevator Company 131
engine: American Standard 132; Atlantic 132; diesel 7, 23; electric 12, 23, 71, 97, 100; Hinkley consolidated 132; Hudson 132; steam 7, 23, 36, 43, 64, 77, 79, 81, 84, 85, 88
engine house   133. See also roundhouse
engineer seniority   64, 110
Enid Railroad Museum   79

F

Fogarty, John (conductor) 25, 29, 130
Fort Smith & Western Railroad (FS&W; aka Footsore & Weary) 35, 36, 71, 81, 82, 83, 84, 85, 86, 87, 88, 89
freight depot 16, 72, 73, 124
Friday Store 6

G

Gold Bond coupon 19
grain elevator 61–63, 73
"Granger Road" 72
Great Depression 35
Griswold, James Levi (engineer) 29
"The Guardsmen" (lawmen Chris Madsen, Heck Thomas, Bill Tilghman) 130
Gulf Railroad Company 20
Gulf, Colorado & Santa Fe Railroad 19
Guss and Coyle's Company 22
Guthrie, John (judge) 20
Guthrie Arts and Humanities Council 49
"Guthrie Daily Ledger" 94
Guthrie Ice & Cold Storage Co. 44
Guthrie Railway Co. (see Guthrie Street Railway)
Guthrie Roundhouse 37
Guthrie Special 132
Guthrie Street Railway (trolley) 71, 96, 97, 98, 99
Guthrie Territorial Museum 47
Guthrie & Western Railway 31

H

Hamilton, J.H. 97
Hamilton-Rankin Hardware Co. 97
Harvey, Fred 115, 116–117
Harvey Girl (waitress) 116–117
Harvey House (restaurants) 105, 116–117
Heartland Flyer 7, 8, 102, 103, 133
Hillsdale Depot 7, 62–63
hopper 63–64
Hotel Ione 107
Humphries, Carl 131

I

Indian Territory 12, 14, 16, 19, 72
inspection and repair report(s) 120–121
Iron Horse 19

J
Jennings, Al (outlaw, actor) 109
"Jim Crow" 132

K
Kansas Citian 132
Kansas City, Mexico & Orient Railroad 17, 63
Kansas City Southern Railway 7, 19, 61
The Katy Flyer (magazine) 89
Katy Historical Society 89
Kingfisher Depot 32, 59, 73
Kiowa Depot 55

L
land claim/stake 14, 16, 112, 130
Land Office 14
Land Rush (1899) 12, 16, 18, 20, 122
Leonhardt, Margaret 115
locomotive: diesel, 23; Mikado 134; Pacific 132, 134; steam 43

M
map/chart: Blanton Junction 48; Guthrie 31, 126; Guthrie Railway 100; Logan County 30; Merrick 56; Peavine line 31, 74; Santa Fe lines 24, 26, 86; Seward Junction 40, 41
marker lamp 134
Marshall Depot 53
Mellon, Andrew 81
Merrick Depot 32, 35, 56, 57, 58
Mikado (see locomotive)
Missouri, Kansas, Texas Railroad (MKT, Katy) 12, 16, 19, 71, 81, 89, 90, 92
Missouri Pacific Railroad 89

mogul 43
motel 28
Mudge Station 46

N
Native Americans (Five Civilized Tribes) 16, 19
Navina Depot/Station 38, 39
Newcomb, "Bittercreek" (outlaw) 130
Nix, Evitt D. (U.S. marshall) 130

O
oil 6, 32, 36, 103
Oklahoma City Railway (later Oklahoma Railway Company) 100
Oklahoma City Train Show 6
Oklahoma Colony Camp 122
Oklahoma Historian Hall of Fame 6
Oklahoma Historical Society 6, 32
Oklahoma Railway Company 12, 75, 81, 97, 100, 101
Oklahoma Statehood Centennial 105, 134
Oklahoma Territory 12, 20, 72, 81, 89

P
Panhandle Sub 55
Parker, Isaac (judge) 130
Passenger Rail Oklahoma (PRO) 103, 105
Pawnee Station 23, 104
Peavine 12, 31, 56. See also Rock Island
Peckham, Ed L. 43
Pullman car 64, 134

R
rail fanning 64

Rail Post Office (RPO)   7
railroad house   118
railroad pass   2
railroad shop   46, 132
railroad yard   50, 63, 64–65, 73, 81, 92
Railway & Locomotive Historical Society   109
Rain, John (engineer)   109
Read, Ezra Hart   6
right(s) of way (ROW)   20
Ripley, Edward P. (president, Santa Fe lines)   31
Roberts, J.H.   32
Rock Island   4, 5, 31–32, 34, 35, 43, 56, 58, 59, 62, 70, 71, 72–73, 75, 92, 103
Rock Island Depot (Station)   22, 59, 72
roundhouse   37, 54, 132
Rouse, Maurice D.   16, 130

S
St. Louis, El Reno & Western Railroad   12, 71, 81, 82, 88
St. Louis & San Francisco Railroad (Frisco)   6, 12, 17, 19, 47, 51, 56, 62, 64, 75, 77, 79, 80, 81, 104
Santa Fe Depot (Station)   6, 20, 47, 62, 124
Santa Fe Railway   7, 8, 11, 12, 18, 20, 23, 24, 26, 28, 31, 35, 37, 43, 44, 52, 60, 61–64, 66, 68, 72, 75, 81, 82, 100, 103, 109, 130, 132–134
Santa Fe Railway Agency/Oklahoma Division (operating hours)   108
Santa Fe Railway Historical & Modeling Society   61
Save Our Depot   113
Seward Depot   40, 41
Shartel, John W.   97
sod house   128
Sooners   12, 14, 16

Southern Kansas Railway   19
Southwest Chief   103
speed (record-breaking)   65, 66, 122–123
speeder   52
Stillwater Central Railroad   23, 60
stockyard   35
streamliner   132
streetcar (see trolley)
surveying   75
switch(er)   6, 62, 65, 106, 132
switch crew   132

T
telegraph   35, 64
Texas Chief (later Lone Star)   7, 63, 66, 103, 117
Thompson, C.M. (conductor)   131
ticket   51
timetable, time card   6, 17, 29, 32, 33, 34, 45, 65, 75, 77
Townsend, C.M. (postal worker)   131
traffic flow   27
train: dinner, 24, 52, 79, 103; football 29; freight 7, 12, 14, 20, 23, 24, 26, 35, 43, 53, 61, 62–63, 105, 134; grain, wheat 7, 61–64; mail 7, 35; passenger 7, 8, 12, 18, 19, 20, 26, 32, 33, 43, 46, 47, 56, 64, 84, 100, 103, 104, 105, 106, 109, 129, 132; stock 28
train order (sheet)   67, 69
trolley   62, 96, 97, 101
turntable (see roundhouse)

U
Union Depot/Station   18, 19, 20, 31
Union Pacific Railroad   72, 89
United Parcel Service (UPS)   64–65

U.S. Geological Survey (USGS)   33, 39, 40, 48
U.S. Navy   100

W
Walsh, Amy   32
The Warbonnet (magazine)   61
water tank   12, 18, 35, 109
Wells Fargo Office   124
"Wheat Capital of the World" (Enid, Oklahoma)   62
whistle   66, 134
Wogan and Calligan (contractors)   31
Wood, Sr. Sylvan R. (photographer)   23
wreck   58
wye   26, 64, 74, 81, 82

Y
Yale Depot Rail Museum   6
Yale Lock Company   6